Cities
Without
Suburbs

Cities Without Suburbs

Second Edition

David Rusk

 Published by The Woodrow Wilson Center Press
Distributed by The Johns Hopkins University Press

Woodrow Wilson Center Special Studies

The Woodrow Wilson Center Press
Editorial Offices
370 L'Enfant Promenade, S.W.
Suite 704
Washington, D.C. 20024-2518 U.S.A.
telephone 202-287-3000, ext. 218

Distributed by:
The Johns Hopkins University Press
Hampden Station
Baltimore, Maryland 21211
Order department telephone 1-800-537-5487

9 8 7 6 5 4

Library of Congress Cataloging in Publication Data

Rusk, David.
    Cities without suburbs / David Rusk. — 2nd ed.
        p.   cm. — (Woodrow Wilson Center special studies)
    Includes bibliographical references (p.   ) and index.
    ISBN 0-943875-74-9 (cloth : alk. paper). — ISBN 0-943875-73-0
    (pbk. : alk. paper)
    1. Urban policy—United States.   2. Metropolitan government—
United States.   3. Metropolitan areas—United States.   I. Title.
II. Series.
HT123.R84   1995   95-23767
307.76'0973—dc20   CIP

To
Delcia,
my wife
and
partner

Contents

Boxes

Preface

"This short book is written for public policymakers. Its intended audience is our new president and his administration, U.S. senators and representatives, state governors, legislators, city and county elected officials—and key staff everywhere who behind the scenes help make American government work. I also wrote the book for thoughtful and concerned citizens who are prepared to think in a different way about what has happened in and around their communities and who will spur their public officials to take decisive action."

This was the audience I targeted in the preface to the first edition of *Cities without Suburbs*. Since its publication in April 1993, *Cities without Suburbs* has clearly had an impact on that audience. Though hardly received on the scale of the latest best-selling novel, the book went through seven printings, encouraging the publishers to request a revised edition. Its themes were reviewed or discussed in over three hundred magazine and newspaper articles and increasingly cited in scholarly works. I have been invited to speak or consult in over sixty metropolitan areas, ranging in size from Jamestown, New York, to New York, New York, covering the country from Jacksonville, Florida, to Seattle, Washington.

If all this sounds too self-congratulatory, I am reminded that there is a tremendous difference between the world of opinion and the world of decision. Has *Cities without Suburbs* really changed anything—anywhere? Are there any communities in this country where life is better as a result of my efforts? The most hopeful answer is "not yet" or, perhaps, "just barely."

Recognizing that few reforms in metropolitan governance have actually occurred as yet, there are two reasons for a second edition of this book. First, I want to sharpen its arguments by including new research and experiences I have had since the first edition was published. Of the new research, most important is an improved way of calculating a city's elasticity, which has caused a revision of the tables in Chapter II and realignment of many cities among elasticity categories in the appendices. Also, I summarize additional research on cost-of-living differentials, long-term change in real income, and concentration of poverty in all metro areas. There are new mini–case studies on building a central city-older suburban coalition in the Minnesota legislature, the impact of township government, integrating public housing children into middle-class schools, and achieving regional tax sharing.

Second, I have almost completely revised my recommendations for federal policy reform in Chapter III. This reflects my experiences in working both with the Clinton administration, particularly the Department of Housing and Urban Development, and with the leadership of the new Republican majorities in the U.S. Congress. Despite continued decline of federal aid to cities, the future or urban America will be brighter if, through key policy changes, the federal government will stop aiding and abetting urban sprawl, abandonment of older communities, and growing economic segregation.

In the first edition, I said that "this book is intended to be argumentative. I have been cautious in neither characterizations nor conclusions. It is not my purpose for each page to be unassailable. The cold, clear light of scholarly criticism may show that I'm a little wrong about details. In terms of the big picture, I believe that I am right." Two years of intensive experiences around the country and further research have reinforced my view of the big picture.

The foundation of this book, first and foremost, is my practical experience—political and managerial—as mayor of Albuquerque from 1977 to 1981. Four years as chief executive of the largest city in New Mexico may, in some readers' opinion, not qualify me to be an expert on what has been happening to America's cities. But Albuquerque is a bigger city—and its city hall runs a bigger city government—than such "big league" cities as Atlanta, Buffalo, Cincinnati, Minneapolis (and St. Paul), Oakland, Pittsburgh, and St. Louis. Within ten or twenty years at most, Albuquerque's population will surpass that of the cities of Boston, Cleveland, Denver, Kansas City, New Orleans, and Washington, D.C.

All this because, as a "central city," Albuquerque is growing, and the others are shrinking! The reason why an Albuquerque grows and an Atlanta, Cleveland, or St. Louis shrinks—what I call a city's "elasticity"—lies at the heart of America's urban problem.

Other practical career experiences shape this book. Before becoming mayor, I spent three years as a state legislator in New

Mexico and five years as a civil rights and antipoverty worker with the Washington Urban League. Also valuable was my federal government experience as the U.S. Manpower Administration's legislative services chief.

In addition, this book is the product of painstaking, hands-on research. Both before and after the first edition's publication, I have passed endless days unearthing data from old census publications. My long backward look over the past four decades forced me to laboriously copy and then enter over 150,000 pieces of information into the database of my personal computer. During 1992, I devoted all my time to researching what has been happening to all of America's 522 central cities in 320 metropolitan areas. This revised edition now incorporates some of my latest research, including further studies of long-term economic growth, cost of living, and poverty.

I originally decided to write *Cities without Suburbs* as an act of hope and faith. I believe that the problem this book addresses—the urban problem—is the toughest issue in American society. It goes right to the heart of the deep-rooted fears about race and social class that have had so much to do with shaping urban America today.

Yet my two years of active involvement in over sixty communities have both sharpened my understanding of this challenge and increased my optimism. The issue is not so much urban poverty overall as *highly concentrated* urban poverty in certain central cities and older suburbs, in poverty-impacted neighborhoods, and among Blacks and Hispanics (as contrasted with non-Hispanic Whites). In urban America, there are 10.8 million poor Whites compared with 6.9 million poor Blacks and 4.8 million poor Hispanics. In a typical metropolitan area, however, three out of four poor Whites live in middle-class neighborhoods scattered widely across the whole area; by contrast, three out of four poor Blacks and two out of three poor Hispanics live in poverty-impacted, inner-city neighborhoods.

Inner-city poverty appears insurmountable because of this very high degree of concentration. Yet America is not some Third World country where the poor are many and the middle class are few. Of every 100 residents of America's metropolitan areas about six are poor and White—and mostly integrated into middle-class society. And of every 100 residents only about six are poor and Black or Hispanic—but much more isolated from middle-class society. I find it hard to believe that middle-class America does not have the capacity to absorb poor Blacks and

Hispanics as it already absorbs most poor Whites. What is lacking too often is not the resources but the political will.

Nevertheless, seen in this regional context, the manageable scale of the problem is one source of my optimism. And I have met and worked with too many concerned and engaged citizens and organizations in the sixty communities that I have visited to believe that the will to change is not emerging as well in many communities.

These may sound like quixotic words in the wake of the 1994 elections, which saw conservative Republicans gain control of both houses of Congress for the first time in forty years. Many liberal commentators have branded the so-called Republican Revolution as "mean-spirited" or "out to punish the poor."

Yet, as Winston Churchill once commented, at the end of the day, the American people will do the right thing—after they have exhausted all other alternatives. I have faith that our political debates, as Abraham Lincoln testified in his first inaugural address, will be "again touched, as surely they will be, by the angels of our better nature." The policy debate must be framed not as a choice between conservative and liberal philosophies, but as a choice between policies that work and policies that do not work. The purpose of *Cities without Suburbs* is to point out what works.

As with the original book, the revised edition will focus primarily on policies that lead to more unified local governance—municipal annexation powers, city-county consolidation, and formal regional government. How local governance is organized helps shape how diverse peoples define themselves as a community. More unified governance leads to a more unified society.

In other books, however, I address in greater detail how in larger, more complex metropolitan areas the myriad of local governments can be brought to act as one government in dealing with critical regional issues. *Baltimore Unbound* (1995) is a detailed case study of the Baltimore metropolitan area, and a new book, commissioned by the Twentieth Century Fund and scheduled for publication in 1997, will examine regional growth management, housing, and revenue-sharing strategies in more detail. The primary purpose of *Cities without Suburbs* is to help us look the urban problem full in the face.

Acknowledgments

Several years ago I conceived this book, but it probably would never have been born without the assistance of Director Charles Blitzer and the Woodrow Wilson International Center for Scholars. For the summer of 1992, the Woodrow Wilson Center invited me to be a Guest Scholar on urban affairs. I am indebted to the Center for its gracious support and for the opportunity to exchange ideas with many stimulating colleagues. In particular, I appreciate the critical guidance from our "urban cluster"—Joe Tulchin, Blair Ruble, and Mary Bullock (all three staff members of the Center); Ed Bergman (University of North Carolina); John Walton (University of California at Davis); and my comrade-in-arms, Hank Savitch (University of Louisville).

I also received invaluable assistance from Daniel Green, my research associate that summer, from the U.S. Census Bureau Library, and from the Business and Economics Division of the Martin Luther King Library in the District of Columbia.

In addition to the friends and colleagues who read and critiqued my work, I am particularly grateful to Dick Rowson, Joseph Brinley, and Carolee Belkin Walker at the Woodrow Wilson Center Press as well as to Barbara de Boinville for patient and professional editing.

Despite my debt to all who have helped me, the responsibility for the book's analysis and recommendations is purely mine.

Finally, I wish to thank my family—my mother, father, and brother, Rich, who were veterans of one book collaboration; Gregory, who sacrificed his Macintosh; Patrick, our computer maven, who set up the initial spreadsheets and provided long-distance technical assistance; Monica and son-in-law, Mark, who constantly encouraged me; and my wife, Delcia, who, having shared my life's experience, has been my most valuable editor and contributor. Their love and support have sustained me.

Introduction: Framing the Issue

To discuss "urban policy" it is helpful to have a common view of the "urban problem." Economists debate urban labor supply, capital availability, and internal and external market opportunities. Housing experts discuss how to ensure adequate, affordable shelter, and transportation planners, how to move people and goods within and beyond urban areas. Public works administrators plan for water and sewer systems, storm drains, and power grids; environmentalists worry about urban air and water quality. Finally, local elected officials argue among themselves (and with their constituents) about how to pay for public wants. Each group sees its area of responsibility as part of the urban problem.

Jobs, housing, streets and highways, water and sewer systems, pollution, and revenues are common issues for urban areas everywhere, but collectively they do not seem to add up to America's urban problem. In fact, compared with most urban populations throughout the world, America does not really have an urban problem as such. Most urban Americans are better employed, better housed, better served by transportation systems and public facilities, and live in better environmental conditions than the rest of the world. America's real urban problem is the racial and economic segregation that has created an underclass in many of America's major urban areas.

Segregating poor urban Blacks and Hispanics has spawned physically decaying, revenue-strapped, poverty-impacted, crime-ridden "inner cities." These inner cities are isolated from their "outer cities"—wealthier, growing, largely White suburbs.

Debate over urban policy has focused on only a handful of America's largest inner cities. By contrast, this book will look at all urban areas and examine in detail more than 100 urban areas with populations of 200,000 or more. Also, by contrast, my focus will be on entire metropolitan areas—cities and suburbs.

This broader perspective will yield, I hope, greater clarity

1

about what has been happening in urban America. There are
lessons to be learned from many urban areas that are rarely analyzed. There are bad lessons to be drawn from areas such as
Harrisburg, Pennsylvania, and Syracuse, New York. There are
success stories to be learned, for example, from Madison, Wisconsin, and my own Albuquerque.

In highly segregated urban areas—no matter how wealthy
areawide—concentrated poverty, welfare dependency, and crime
compound each other, and inner cities are failing. In more integrated urban areas—even when poorer areawide—poverty, dependency, and crime lack critical mass, and the cities are
succeeding.

In about half of the country's large urban areas, social and
economic inequities are severe. In the other half, however, good
timing, good luck, and good public policy—which come to focus
in what I call a city's "elasticity"—have combined to create more
successful communities for Whites, Blacks, and Hispanics alike.
In short, half of America's large urban areas needs to take some
pointers from the other half about what works. Conversely, the
other half needs to learn to avoid the path of failure shown by
the first.

In the first chapter, I derive twenty-four "lessons" and four
"laws" from what has been happening in urban America since
World War II. The statistical analysis typically begins with the
1950 census and ends with the 1990 census. The first four lessons
stated in Chapter I are supported by data drawn from the 320
metropolitan areas in the United States. Thereafter, to give the
reader a more tangible feel for my observations, I illustrate the
remaining general lessons by contrasting seven pairs of specific
metropolitan areas: Houston and Detroit, Columbus and Cleveland, Nashville and Louisville, Indianapolis and Milwaukee, Albuquerque and Syracuse, Madison and Harrisburg, Raleigh and
Richmond.

In Chapter II, "Characteristics of Metropolitan Areas," I take
the lessons stated and illustrated in Chapter I and divide most of
the large urban areas into five broad categories. For each of these
broad categories, I then restate the key data used for Chapter I.

In Chapter III, I discuss strategies for "stretching" cities. These
strategies are framed for action at the local, state, and federal levels. There is not a single strategy that, in conventional political
terms, would be easy to accomplish. Our society has spent
decades building up this mess. There will be no easy solutions.

I believe that adopting these strategies—creating "cities without suburbs"—can profoundly transform the long-term outlook for failing central cities and help re-energize American society.

Chapter IV presents my conclusions and specific recommendations. Ultimately, reform of our cities must arise from broad-based citizen movements for change. Building popular movements is more art than science. Success lies more in the doing than in the telling.

Finally, I revisit some key ideas and acknowledge some additional considerations in an Afterword.

A clarifying comment on terminology. I often told Albuquerque audiences that New Mexico is one of the few places where a Puccini, a Pulaski, and a Goldstein could all be called "Anglo." Throughout the book, when I refer to "White," I mean "Anglo"—that is, non-Hispanic whites. And, contrary to commonly accepted editorial style, I will refer to Whites, Blacks, and Hispanics with coequal capital letters. I do not mean to slight either the problems or achievements of urban Asian and Native Americans by not focusing on them. From my analysis, however, it is only around Whites, Blacks, and Hispanics that social and political attitudes in America revolve with sufficient force and magnitude to shape patterns of urban growth.

Chapter I

Lessons from Urban America

Despite the romance of the frontier, the true land of opportunity in America for over 150 years has been the cities. From farms and foreign lands, urban immigrants flocked into the cities, seeking better schools, better jobs, better health care—in short, a better life. What lessons can be drawn from a broad look at what has been happening in urban America over the last forty years?

Lesson 1: The real city is the total metropolitan area—city and suburb.

At the end of World War II, urban America was still the inner cities. There were hardly any outer cities. The suburban movement was just starting. The country's biggest cities were booming and bursting at the seams. Drawn by the war industries, millions had left farms and small towns to pack into the cities.

In 1950 almost 70 percent of the population of 168 metropolitan areas lived in 193 central cities. (For an explanation of Census Bureau terms, see Box 1.1.) City residents attended the same city school system. They used the city parks and libraries. They rode city buses, streetcars, and subways to blue- and white-collar jobs within the city or, occasionally, to nearby factories. They fought for control of the same city hall. Although there were often fierce rivalries among ethnic and racial groups, common public institutions were unifying forces (except in the segregated South).

Today the situation is reversed. By 1990 over 60 percent of the population of 320 metropolitan areas lived in suburbs. Equally as important, suburbs no longer simply served as bedroom communities for workers with city-based jobs. By 1990 a majority of jobs in metro areas were located in suburbs as well.

Box 1.1 What Is a Metropolitan Area?

According to the U.S. Census Bureau, a "metropolitan area" (Metropolitan Statistical Area, MSA, or metro area) is "a geographic area consisting of a large population nucleus together with adjacent communities which have a high degree of economic and social integration with that nucleus." In short, a metro area is a city and its suburbs.

Each metro area must include a "central city" that, with contiguous, densely settled territory, constitutes a Census Bureau-defined urbanized area of at least 50,000 people. If the largest city has fewer than 50,000 people, the area must have a total population of at least 100,000.

In 1910 the Census Bureau first introduced "metropolitan districts." Since then it has used many different methodologies to define metro areas, but by 1950 it had settled on using entire counties as the building blocks of metro areas. Counties outside of the "central county" in which the "central city" is located are added based on commuting patterns of workers into the central city or central county.

In recent decades the Census Bureau has recognized additional central cities beyond the historic focal points of many metro areas. Now there are 522 central cities in 320 metro areas. A metro area's title may include up to three central cities, such as "Tampa-St. Petersburg-Clearwater FL MSA."

Seventeen of the largest urban regions are designated as Consolidated Metropolitan Statistical Areas (CMSAs) composed of two or more Primary Metropolitan Statistical Areas (PMSAs). In New England (where counties are not primary local governments), the Census Bureau for statistical purposes has designated New England County Metropolitan Areas (NECMAs).

In this book the basic unit of analysis will be a MSA, PMSA, or NECMA. In metro areas of more than one central city, only the first named city will be treated as the central city (for example, Tampa for Tampa-St. Petersburg-Clearwater, Florida).

All metro areas will be analyzed as they were defined as of June 30, 1989. A metro area's population in 1950 will include the populations in 1950 of all counties considered part of the metro area in 1990 rather than how the metro area was conceived under 1950 conditions.

The traditional city no longer is "the place to be" to find a better life. In fact, housing, jobs, schools, and services are worse in many inner cities than they are in the neighboring suburbs. Any attack on urban social and economic problems must treat suburb and city as indivisible parts of a whole.

Lesson 2: Most of America's Blacks, Hispanics, and Asians live in urban areas.

Forty years ago the country's 15 million Blacks were still substantially rural and southern, although a tremendous migration into cities north and south had been under way since the Great Depression. Similarly, most of the country's Hispanics were scattered in rural areas and small cities located largely throughout the Southwest. Asian Americans, always an urban people, were heavily concentrated in West Coast cities.

In 1950 America's population was about 86 to 87 percent White and 13 to 14 percent minority (including Native Americans).[1] Forty years later America is 27 percent minority, and over 80 percent of all minorities live in metropolitan areas. In fact, a majority of all Blacks, Hispanics, and Asians lives in just thirty metropolitan areas.[2]

Today minorities as well as opportunity are concentrated in urban areas. Social and economic equality is a goal that can be achieved only by what happens in urban areas.

Lesson 3: Since World War II, all urban growth has been low-density, suburban style.

The 1950 census was the high watermark for most of America's big cities. Of the twelve largest cities, ten (all except New York and Los Angeles) hit their population peaks in the 1950 census.

Thereafter, Washington, Wall Street, Detroit, Hollywood, and Madison Avenue made middle-class families an offer they could not refuse: the American Dream. Sustained economic growth, cheap home mortgages, affordable private cars, and federally subsidized highways—all touted on big screens and small—made that dream house with its own yard, quiet neighborhood, local school, and nearby shopping possible for millions of families. Compared with staying put in many city neighborhoods, suburbia was a bargain. Urban America became Suburban America.

Everyone knows this. What is not always recognized is how universal this pattern has been in postwar America.

A key measure is "population density." Population density measures how many people live per square mile. What has happened to population densities in America depends on the frame of reference.

Time-traveling from the 1790s, Daniel Boone would find the whole country intolerably densely populated in the 1990s with its 245 million people.[3] Long-time residents of rural areas and small towns may well feel that the countryside is getting "too crowded" today with new suburban subdivisions springing up around them.

But within America's 522 central cities, population density has declined by 50 percent![4] From 5,873 persons per square mile in 1950, overall density dropped to 2,937 persons per square mile in 1990. And that happened almost everywhere—in big cities and small. In 1950, for example, there were thirty-eight cities with densities of 10,000 or more persons per square mile. Over the next forty years all thirty-eight lost density. By 1990 there were only fifteen cities with densities of 10,000 or more persons per square mile.

During this period 107 of 522 central cities actually increased their population densities, but almost all of these were well below the average national density in 1950. In effect, most were thinly populated areas waiting to become more populated, but still low-density, "cities."

Only five cities with above-average densities in 1950 and a half dozen others that had densities just below average actually increased their densities. All were targets of Hispanic immigration.

Miami, Miami Beach, and Hialeah, Florida, were all centers of Cuban and Central American immigration in which the Hispanic population comprised 62 percent, 47 percent, and 88 percent, respectively, by 1990.

The Pacific Rim's Ellis Island was the greater Los Angeles area, as Hispanic and Asian immigrants filled Los Angeles, Long Beach, Burbank, Pasadena, Pomona, and, in neighboring Orange County, Anaheim and Santa Ana. In fact, one-third of

Los Angeles County's population in 1990 was foreign-born—half having arrived in the past decade!

Other immigration focused on the greater New York area, the traditional port of entry. Immigrants cushioned New York City against greater population loss (only –7 percent between 1950 and 1990). Immigrants also kept smaller cities like Paterson, Elizabeth, and Perth Amboy, New Jersey, filled up to higher than usual densities.

In short, the only cities in America that swam against the suburban stream were cities swimming with the immigrant stream. A certain natural clustering of new immigrants, large families (including extended families), low incomes, and a degree of anti-Hispanic or anti-Asian discrimination in neighboring communities combined to sustain growing densities in these port-of-entry cities. Everywhere else, most middle-class, White Americans for the past forty years have chosen to raise young families in low-density communities rather than high-density cities.

Lesson 4: For a city's population to grow, the city must be "elastic."

Think of a city as a map drawn on a rubber sheet. If there is a great deal of vacant land within existing city limits, that city's population density is low. The city has room for new population growth by filling in undeveloped land. In effect, the rubber sheet map is slack. Facing growth opportunities, the city is still elastic within its boundaries because of its low population density. It can stretch upward to accommodate new growth.[5]

On the other hand, what if the city is already densely populated? There is little or no vacant land to develop. Its rubber sheet map is stretched taut within its existing boundaries.

That high-density city cannot become more dense. (That is not a lifestyle that most postwar, middle-class families "buy.") The high-density city's only path to growth is to expand its boundaries. It must stretch the edges of its rubber sheet map to take in new territory. It must become more elastic outward rather than upward.

The most common method by which a city acquires new territory is annexation. Sometimes, a city annexes undeveloped land. More often, an annexation brings in an existing community. Stretching the edges of the municipal map often creates tension—outside resistance from those to be annexed and inside resistance from a city's current residents. Annexation is not always easy.

How much did cities utilize each mechanism—filling in vacant land and annexing additional territory? Only about 20 percent of all cities actually increased their densities. For many other cities, however, in-fill development was combined with boundary expansion (which often tended to mask the degree of in-fill development).

Boundary expansion contributed most to municipal elasticity. Between 1950 and 1990 more than four-fifths of the 522 central cities expanded their boundaries by 10 percent or more. The municipal expansion champion was Anchorage, Alaska. By absorbing its entire surrounding borough, the city of Anchorage grew from 12.5 square miles to 1,697.7 square miles (13,482 percent)! Overall, the 522 central cities expanded from 10,513 square miles to 27,728 square miles (164 percent, or 149 percent if Anchorage's massive land grab is discounted).

On the threshold of the era of the suburban lifestyle, the cities with the greatest elasticity had vacant city land to develop *and* the political and legal tools to annex new land. These I will call "elastic cities." At the other end of the spectrum were the "inelastic cities"—typically, older cities already built out at higher than average densities and, for a variety of reasons, unable or unwilling to expand their city limits.

This pattern of urban development is sufficiently universal (at least, in America) to embolden me to state the first law of urban dynamics: *only elastic cities grow.*

This concept of a city's elasticity is the central idea of this book. Why have some cities been elastic and others have not? What are the demographic, economic, and social consequences of inelasticity? If being an elastic city is essential to economic, social, and fiscal health, what can be done to make inelastic cities elastic again or, at least, to benefit as if they were elastic?

Summary data for all metro areas support the first four lessons I have presented. The succeeding lessons are best illustrated by contrasting specific metro areas that I have paired: Detroit-Houston, Columbus-Cleveland, Nashville-Louisville, Indianapolis-Milwaukee, Albuquerque-Syracuse, Madison-Harrisburg, and Raleigh-Richmond. At first glance several of the metro areas paired may seem to have nothing in common. All pairs, however, have been matched in terms of two key characteristics. First, from 1950 to 1990 the metro areas in each pair added roughly equal numbers of new residents as measured by net growth of the metro population and by new-home buyers (Table 1.1). (How "new-home buyers" is derived is discussed on pages 14–15.) Second, by 1990 the metro areas of each pair had roughly the same percentage of Black population metrowide (Table 1.2).

Although the metro areas in each pair are equivalent in new-home buyers and percentage of Black population, the relative elasticity of the principal central cities in each pair is not the same. The more elastic city or area is listed first; the less elastic city or area is listed second. (For example, Houston is more elastic than Detroit.)[6]

TABLE 1.1
EACH PAIR OF METRO AREAS HAS ABOUT THE
SAME NUMBER OF NEW-HOME BUYERS

Metro area	New-home buyers 1950–90
Houston, Tex.	2,400,986
Detroit, Mich.	1,957,962
Columbus, Ohio	648,617
Cleveland, Ohio	707,740
Nashville, Tenn.	483,118
Louisville, Ky.	417,691
Indianapolis, Ind.	522,700
Milwaukee, Wis.	427,242
Albuquerque, N. Mex.	334,904
Syracuse, N.Y.	251,473
Madison, Wis.	197,728
Harrisburg, Pa.	226,448
Raleigh, N.C.	431,615
Richmond, Va.	429,830

TABLE 1.2
Each Pair of Metro Areas Has about the Same
Percentage of Blacks in the Population

Metro area	Percentage of Blacks in the metro population
Houston, Tex.	19%
Detroit, Mich.	21
Columbus, Ohio	12
Cleveland, Ohio	19
Nashville, Tenn.	15
Louisville, Ky.	13
Indianapolis, Ind.	14
Milwaukee, Wis.	14
Albuquerque, N. Mex.	3
Syracuse, N.Y.	6
Madison, Wis.	3
Harrisburg, Pa.	7
Raleigh, N.C.	25
Richmond, Va.	29

Lesson 5: Almost all metro areas have grown.

It is easy to label Detroit, Cleveland, and Milwaukee "dying Frostbelt areas" and Houston, Raleigh, and Albuquerque "booming Sunbelt areas." The truth is, however, that the populations of all of these Frostbelt areas have grown as *total metropolitan areas*. In fact, the populations of most metropolitan areas have grown over the past four decades.[7]

Table 1.3 presents the metro population growth of the seven pairs of metro areas. Metro areas containing elastic cities have had higher growth rates than metro areas with inelastic cities. These metro areas began at lower population levels. However, in 1990 the metro areas containing the inelastic cities were still somewhat more populous (with the exception of Nashville, which had edged ahead of Louisville). The inelastic areas began at much higher population levels and added to that base.

Growth rates, of course, are a function of how much is added to how large an initial base. Each additional resident contributes

TABLE 1.3
ALMOST ALL METRO AREAS HAVE GROWN

Metro area	Metro population			Percentage change 1950–90
	1950	1990	Change 1950–90	
Houston, Tex.	900,951	3,301,937	2,400,986	174%
Detroit, Mich.	3,245,981	4,382,299	1,136,318	35
Columbus, Ohio	728,802	1,377,419	648,617	89
Cleveland, Ohio	1,532,574	1,831,122	298,548	19
Nashville, Tenn.	501,908	985,026	483,118	96
Louisville, Ky.	635,037	952,662	317,625	50
Indianapolis, Ind.	727,122	1,249,822	522,700	72
Milwaukee, Wis.	1,014,211	1,432,149	417,938	41
Albuquerque, N. Mex.	145,673	480,577	334,904	230
Syracuse, N.Y.	465,114	659,864	194,750	42
Madison, Wis.	169,357	367,085	197,728	117
Harrisburg, Pa.	398,706	587,986	189,280	47
Raleigh, N.C.	303,865	735,480	431,615	142
Richmond, Va.	463,064	865,640	402,576	87

to a higher rate of growth where there is a smaller initial population base than a larger initial population base. Thus, the rates of population growth among elastic areas (72 percent to 230 percent) were much higher than growth rates among inelastic areas (19 percent to 87 percent).

Do great disparities in *rates* of population growth make a difference? Of course they do. For an area to double its population (Columbus, Nashville, Madison) or triple its population (Houston, Albuquerque) creates a different business climate, a different community climate, even a "boom town" psychology, than exist in an area that grows more slowly.

However, the spectacular rates of population growth of some metro areas have obscured the fact that less spectacularly expanding areas have added hundreds of thousands or millions of new residents. For example, from 1950 to 1990 the Houston metro area added 2.4 million people (net), but the Detroit metro area added 1.1 million people (net) as well. In addition, metro Houston's and metro Detroit's growth were much closer in terms of numbers of families looking for new homes—the key to how local jurisdictions grow within the same metro area.

Lesson 6: Some central cities have grown; others have shrunk.

Central to the urban problem is *how* different metro areas have grown. As Table 1.4 shows, the inelastic cities suffered catastrophic population losses. Metro population growth occurred entirely in suburbs outside these cities' boundaries. In sharp contrast, the elastic cities grew substantially.

Table 1.1 earlier summarized the effect of these sharply contrasting growth patterns (1950–90) in terms of new-home buyers. How is this concept of "new-home buyers" derived?

Since household sizes have fallen throughout America (except in cities with recent immigration), any additional population must be accommodated in new housing, typically in new

TABLE 1.4
SOME CENTRAL CITIES HAVE GROWN;
OTHERS HAVE SHRUNK

Metro area	City population		Change 1950–90	Percentage change 1950–90
	1950	1990		
Houston, Tex.	596,163	1,630,553	1,034,390	174%
Detroit, Mich.	1,849,568	1,027,924	−821,644	−44
Columbus, Ohio	375,901	632,910	257,009	68
Cleveland, Ohio	914,808	505,616	−409,192	−45
Nashville, Tenn.	174,307	488,374	314,067	180
Louisville, Ky.	369,129	269,063	−100,066	−27
Indianapolis, Ind.	427,173	731,327	304,154	71
Milwaukee, Wis.	637,392	628,088	−9,304	−1
Albuquerque, N. Mex.	96,815	384,736	287,921	297
Syracuse, N.Y.	220,583	163,860	−56,723	−26
Madison, Wis.	96,056	191,282	95,226	99
Harrisburg, Pa.	89,544	52,376	−37,168	−42
Raleigh, N.C.	65,679	207,951	142,272	217
Richmond, Va.	230,310	203,056	−27,254	−12

subdivisions. For an elastic area (Houston or Columbus, for example) "new-home buyers" is the same as net metro population growth. (The calculation of new-home buyers includes all household members.) For an inelastic area, however, new homes must be provided for newcomers to the metro area and for current residents moving from the city to the suburbs. For an inelastic area "new-home buyers" is net metro population growth plus the central city's net loss of population. For an inelastic area "new-home buyers" is identical to suburban population growth. I have resisted, however, labeling it "suburban growth" because city and suburb potentially competed to house that population.

How well different cities succeeded in that competition is the heart of the issue. For example, the "booming" Houston area had to accommodate 2,400,986 million residents in new housing, while the "dying" Detroit area had to provide new housing for 1,957,962 (Table 1.1).

Lesson 7: Low-density cities can grow through in-fill; high-density cities cannot.

What was the situation of our sample cities in 1950 as the American Dream picked up momentum? The average density for all 522 central cities in 1950 was 5,873 persons per square mile. Albuquerque and Houston were well below the national average (Table 1.5). They would have accommodated some additional growth within existing city limits. Nashville might have had a little "room at the inn" as well. But even Raleigh, Richmond, and Madison appear by 1950 to have surpassed the density standards associated with the emerging American Dream.

No city after 1950 expanded beyond 5,000 persons per square mile except for cities with Hispanic immigration mentioned above; New Britain and New London, Connecticut (small coastal cities that just edged past the 5,000 per square mile mark); and seven booming college towns—Annapolis, Maryland (U.S. Naval Academy), Davis (University of California), East Lansing (Michigan State), Evanston, Illinois (Northwestern University), New Brunswick, New Jersey (Rutgers University), State College (Penn State), and West Lafayette, Indiana (Purdue). If city planners in 1950 had had crystal balls, they would have seen that any city with a density of 5,000 or more persons per square

TABLE 1.5
LOW-DENSITY CITIES CAN GROW THROUGH IN-FILL;
HIGH-DENSITY CITIES CANNOT

Metro area	City density (persons per square mile) 1950	City density as a percentage of national average density, 1950
Houston, Tex.	3,726	63%
Detroit, Mich.	13,249	226
Columbus, Ohio	9,541	162
Cleveland, Ohio	12,197	208
Nashville, Tenn.	4,333	74
Louisville, Ky.	9,251	158
Indianapolis, Ind.	7,739	132
Milwaukee, Wis.	12,748	217
Albuquerque, N. Mex.	2,021	34
Syracuse, N.Y.	8,719	148
Madison, Wis.	6,237	106
Harrisburg, Pa.	14,213	208
Raleigh, N.C.	5,971	102
Richmond, Va.	6,208	106

mile would have to look for new land, new immigrants, or new college students to add to its population.

Lesson 8: Elastic cities expand their city limits; inelastic cities do not.

Elastic cities did not just fill up vacant areas within existing city limits. They expanded their city limits aggressively (Table 1.6). Houston, Columbus, Albuquerque, Madison, and Raleigh grew through aggressive annexation of surrounding areas. After the earlier pace of annexation had slowed, the city of Nashville and the city of Indianapolis expanded dramatically through consolidation with their home counties to create new, unified governments.

By contrast, almost without exception, inelastic cities entered the postwar growth era locked within their existing boundaries.

TABLE 1.6
ELASTIC CITIES EXPAND THEIR CITY LIMITS;
INELASTIC CITIES DO NOT

Metro area	City area (square miles)		Percentage change
	1950	1990	1950–1990
Houston, Tex.	160	540	237%
Detroit, Mich.	139	139	0
Columbus, Ohio	39	191	385
Cleveland, Ohio	75	77	3
Nashville, Tenn.	22	473	2,051
Louisville, Ky.	40	62	56
Indianapolis, Ind.	55	362	555
Milwaukee, Wis.	50	96	92
Albuquerque, N. Mex.	48	132	176
Syracuse, N.Y.	25	25	0
Madison, Wis.	15	58	275
Harrisburg, Pa.	6	8	29
Raleigh, N.C.	11	88	550
Richmond, Va.	37	60	62

The city limits of Detroit and Syracuse did not budge. The city of Cleveland added only two square miles, as did the city of Harrisburg. (Harrisburg's proportional growth, adding roughly one-third to its 6.3 square miles, might look significant, but the effect was minuscule within a 1,991-square-mile metro area.)

Lesson 9: When a city stops growing, it starts shrinking.

In the early postwar period, Milwaukee, Louisville, and Richmond continued to expand in population and in area (by forty-six, twenty-two, and twenty-three square miles, respectively). Between 1950 and 1960 Milwaukee almost doubled its area and added over 100,000 new residents (about 16 percent growth). Then, as annexation stopped, Milwaukee peaked out. Since its 1960 peak Milwaukee has lost all of that added population. In 1990 its population was slightly below its 1950 level.

Box 1.2 New York City, 1790–1990

My analysis has focused on different cities' "elasticity" amid metro growth over the past forty years, but *all* cities were elastic in their youth. New York City serves as a historical microcosm for urban development patterns everywhere.

In 1790 the city of New York, located on the tip of Manhattan Island, was the country's largest city, surpassing Philadelphia, Boston, and Baltimore. It had 33,131 residents. Barely 16,000 people were scattered in villages and farms in the surrounding boroughs (about fifty people per square mile).

By 1890 the city of New York had packed 1.4 million residents onto Manhattan Island. Linked to the city of New York by the Brooklyn Bridge, the city of Brooklyn was the Phoenix of the nineteenth century, increasing its population twentyfold between 1840 and 1890. The other boroughs, however, were still relatively lightly populated.[1]

In 1898 New York's state legislature created a new New York City by combining the five boroughs and abolishing all other municipal governments, such as the city of Brooklyn. This legislative act, approved over fierce lobbying opposition from wealthy suburbanites in Brooklyn, created the world's largest city (3.4 million in 1900) and the country's first metropolitan government.

Packed with new European immigrants, the old city of New York (Manhattan) had been approaching its capacity. It would still grow another 23 percent in population, but would peak out by 1910. Consolidation made the city of New York elastic again, above all through acquiring more than 200 square miles of lightly settled land in the Bronx, Queens, and Staten Island.

For the next fifty years much of New York City's "suburban" growth occurred within its own city limits. Brooklyn grew another 135 percent, peaking at 2.3 million in 1950. The Bronx grew 625 percent (to 1.5 million) before flattening out in 1950. Queens grew 1,200 percent, finally peaking in 1970 at 2.0 million. Now approaching 400,000 residents, Staten Island's growth has not yet stopped. These earlier "suburbs" may have been subway-and-

---

In similar fashion Louisville and Richmond continued to grow in population while geographic expansion was under way. Louisville added 6 percent until 1960; Richmond, about 8 percent until 1970. Then, when geographic expansion halted, their populations began dropping. The drop in Louisville was pretrolley suburbs rather than the auto-based suburbs of the postwar decades, but they were suburbs all the same.

When the Census Bureau in 1910 conceived of metropolitan districts, it designated New York City as the hub of northern New Jersey (Newark and Jersey City) and Westchester County. New York City constituted over 80 percent of the population of this region. Since then the definition of greater New York has expanded slowly. By 1950 New York City was still 61 percent of the region's population.

Thereafter, the suburban movement blossomed beyond New York's city limits. Nassau and Suffolk counties exploded to 2.6 million people by 1970. Fairfield County, Connecticut, doubled to 828,000 by 1990, drawing off many of Manhattan's richest executives and corporate headquarters. Commuting patterns extended the greater New York area far down into central New Jersey. The counties there doubled and tripled in population.

For five decades, while New York City was largely *its own suburbs*, it was one of the most successful urban communities. New York City's schools, hospitals, and city services were among the nation's best. With all of its warts, New York City was a great magnet for those seeking a better life—and it largely delivered!

But 1950 was the watershed. From 1900 to 1950, New York City captured over 50 percent of its suburban growth; after 1950 it contributed −13 percent to its suburban growth. By 1990 New York City only accounted for 41 percent of regional population.

When it was truly a metro government, New York City was enormously successful. When it slipped into being the central city of a metropolitan region expanding far beyond its borders, its fabled problems began. New York City needs another "Generation of 1898."

1. In 1890 the population densities of New York City's future boroughs were Manhattan, 64,629 people per square mile; Brooklyn, 11,019; the Bronx, 2,049; Queens, 770; and Staten Island, 857. Their 1890 population densities would have ranked the latter three boroughs in the lowest 10 percent of all "suburbanizing" communities sixty years later.

cipitous (−31 percent, from its 1960 peak), while Richmond's population erosion has been more gradual (−19 percent, from its 1970 peak). Richmond's population is now below its 1950 level, while Louisville has turned its population clock back to the 1920s!

Lesson 10: Elastic cities "capture" suburban growth; inelastic cities "contribute" to suburban growth.

As I have shown, all postwar growth has been suburban style, low-density development emphasizing detached, single-family homes. Elastic cities had large inventories of undeveloped land or were able to annex either undeveloped land or new subdivisions. They captured much of this suburban-style growth within their own municipal boundaries.

Inelastic cities could not grow either through in-fill or annexation. They could not compete with new suburbs in offering the desired suburban-style model for family life. Incapable of capturing a share of suburban-type development, inelastic cities actually contributed White, middle-class families to the new suburbs. In recent years in areas such as Washington, D.C., and Atlanta, a rapidly growing Black middle class has moved to the suburbs as well.

Table 1.7 sums up the effect in terms of a city's "capture or contribute" percentage. The "capture or contribute" percentage is calculated by dividing a city's net population growth by the area's new-home buyers. In effect, I am calculating the score in a city's competition with its suburbs for middle-class families.

Houston captured 43 percent of its new-home buyers, while Detroit contributed –42 percent to the suburbs' new-home buyers. Columbus captured 40 percent, Cleveland contributed –58 percent, and so forth down the list. (Milwaukee and Richmond have broken about even to this point, but are playing out losing hands unless they can radically change their cards.)

These metro areas illustrate my first law of urban dynamics: only elastic cities grow. But the first law begs a key question. Why did some cities stop expanding their city limits while other cities continued to grow?

Lesson 11: Bad state laws can hobble cities.

State laws differ concerning the power they give municipalities to expand. In New England, for example, the political map has long been set—in some cases since colonial times. New England state laws do not even provide for municipal annexation. In other regions state laws attach conditions that can severely limit a municipality's practical ability to annex additional territory.

TABLE 1.7
ELASTIC CITIES "CAPTURE" SUBURBAN GROWTH;
INELASTIC CITIES "CONTRIBUTE" TO SUBURBAN GROWTH

Metro area	City population change 1950–90	Metro new-home buyers 1950–90	City capture/ contribute percentage
Houston, Tex.	1,034,390	2,400,986	43%
Detroit, Mich.	–821,644	1,957,962	–42
Columbus, Ohio	257,009	648,617	40
Cleveland, Ohio	–409,192	707,740	–58
Nashville, Tenn.	314,067	483,118	65
Louisville, Ky.	–100,066	417,691	–24
Indianapolis, Ind.	304,154	522,700	58
Milwaukee, Wis.	–9,304	427,242	–2
Albuquerque, N. Mex.	287,921	334,904	86
Syracuse, N.Y.	–56,723	251,473	–23
Madison, Wis.	95,206	197,728	48
Harrisburg, Pa.	–37,168	226,448	–16
Raleigh, N.C.	142,272	431,615	33
Richmond, Va.	–27,254	429,830	–6

Annexation may be allowed only upon voluntary petition by property owners. Often an affirmative vote of affected land owners is required (or even approval by voters in the annexing municipality). Such restrictions on annexation authority are found most often in the Northeast and Midwest.

Table 1.8 summarizes a 1971 study of different cities' annexation powers and constraints. Raleigh's continuous expansion was guaranteed by North Carolina's liberal annexation laws; it had the power—even the obligation—to annex urbanizing areas regardless of property owners' desires. Texas also allowed cities such as Houston to annex unincorporated areas by unilateral council action. Albuquerque's annexations had to be unanimously approved by affected property owners, but the economics of city water and sewer services motivated large land developers to seek annexation.

Pennsylvania, however, had no annexation laws; Harrisburg's expansion was dependent upon negotiating mergers with surrounding boroughs and municipalities (a politically difficult and

TABLE 1.8
BAD STATE LAWS CAN HOBBLE CITIES

Metro area	Municipal annexation			Approval by voters		
	Authorized by state law	Begun by property owner petition	Begun by city council action	Within annexed area	Within annexing city	Approval by county government
Houston, Tex.	Yes	Yes	Yes	No	No	No
Detroit, Mich.	Yes	Yes	[No]	[Yes]	[Yes]	No
Columbus, Ohio	Yes	Yes	Yes	[Yes]	No	[Yes]
Cleveland, Ohio	Yes	Yes	Yes	[Yes]	No	[Yes]
Nashville, Tenn.	Yes	Yes	Yes	[Yes]	[Yes]	No
Louisville, Ky.	Yes	No	Yes	No	No	No
Indianapolis, Ind.	Yes	Yes	Yes	No	No	No
Milwaukee, Wis.	Yes	Yes	[No]	[Yes]	No	No
Albuquerque, N. Mex.	Yes	Yes	Yes	[Yes]	No	No
Syracuse, N.Y.	Yes	Yes	[No]	[Yes]	No	No
Madison, Wis.	Yes	Yes	[No]	[Yes]	No	No
Harrisburg, Pa.	No	N/A	N/A	N/A	N/A	N/A
Raleigh, N.C.	Yes	Yes	Yes	No	No	No
Richmond, Va.	Yes	Yes	Yes	No	No	[Yes]

Note: Adverse requirements are highlighted by brackets.

procedurally cumbersome task). Kentucky's laws were pro-annexation, but also provided a poison pill—ready self-incorporation of small subdivisions facing annexation. After ninety-three suburban micro-municipalities had been organized, Louisville negotiated a no more annexation/no more incorporation truce in return for a tax-sharing "Compact" with Jefferson County. In 1979 the Virginia General Assembly insulated urban counties from further annexations by "independent cities" such as Richmond.

Lesson 12: Neighbors can trap cities.

In some states a municipality cannot expand beyond its home county. By 1950 a few inelastic cities in America had largely filled up small home counties. Other inelastic cities had been transformed into their own counties or into "independent cities" with boundaries that could not expand.[8] By contrast, most elastic cities are located in counties that are geographically much larger; small central cities have room to grow very large.

In all states, however, one municipality cannot annex property within another municipality, regardless of the disparity in size. This can be the most insurmountable barrier to annexation.

A central city's expansion can be blocked by competing municipalities. Many older cities became gradually surrounded by smaller cities, towns, and villages. Newer central cities often faced only farmland, swamp, or sagebrush.

Table 1.9 shows the "elbowroom" each of the sample cities had in 1950. No city had come close to filling up its home county; municipal areas ranged from 1 percent to 23 percent of home-county areas. Detroit, however was bounded by the Detroit River (an international boundary) and fifteen municipalities enclosing 75 percent of its city limits. Cleveland was completely hemmed in by Lake Erie on the north, and by twenty smaller municipalities ringing its city limits. Regardless of state laws, Detroit and Cleveland had nowhere to grow. By contrast, Columbus annexed aggressively, driven by two strategic goals: to become the most populous city in Ohio and never to allow itself to become completely surrounded by incorporated suburbs.

As evidenced by the growth in home-county populations outside the city limits, there was certainly room for population expansion within home counties in 1950 (even around Detroit and Cleveland).[9] Wayne County, for example, added 498,046 new residents outside of Detroit, while Cuyahoga County added 431,800 outside of Cleveland. Both Detroit and Cleveland, however, were blocked from capturing any of that growth. All growth occurred in suburban municipalities or in outlying unincorporated areas blocked off by the *cordon sanitaire* of suburban towns and villages.

Lesson 13: Old cities are complacent; young cities are ambitious.

Certainly one clear distinction between elastic and inelastic cities is age: elastic cities are younger than inelastic cities. Table 1.10 lists the census at which each city first exceeded the 100,000 population milestone.

On the average the inelastic cities passed 100,000 or more residents around 1890, while the elastic cities did not reach that milestone until about 1930. The "average" of 1930, however,

Table 1.9
Most Cities Had Room to Grow between 1950 and 1990

City	Home county	City area as a percentage of home-county area		Percentage of city limits enclosed by other municipalities 1950	Balance of home-county population growth 1950–90	Percentage change in home-county population 1950–90
		1950	1990			
Houston, Tex.	Harris	9%	31%	10%	976,824	464%
Detroit, Mich.	Wayne	23	23	75	498,046	85
Columbus, Ohio	Franklin	7	35	15	201,018	91
Cleveland, Ohio	Cuyahoga	17	17	100	431,800	87
Nashville, Tenn.	Davidson	4	94	1	–125,041	–85
Louisville, Ky.	Jefferson	10	16	30	280,338	243
Indianapolis, Ind.	Marion	14	91	25	–58,772	–47
Milwaukee, Wis.	Milwaukee	21	40	25	97,532	42
Albuquerque, N. Mex.	Bernalillo	4	11	0	46,983	96
Syracuse, N.Y.	Onondaga	3	3	10	183,977	152
Madison, Wis.	Dane	1	5	20	102,522	140
Harrisburg, Pa.	Dauphin	1	1	20	77,197	71
Raleigh, N.C.	Wake	1	11	0	144,658	204
Richmond, Va.	Ind. City	N/A	N/A	0	N/A	N/A

TABLE 1.10
INELASTIC CITIES ARE OLDER THAN ELASTIC CITIES

City	Census when the population exceeded 100,000
Houston, Tex.	1920
Detroit, Mich.	1880
Columbus, Ohio	1900
Cleveland, Ohio	1880
Nashville, Tenn.	1910
Louisville, Ky.	1870
Indianapolis, Ind.	1890
Milwaukee, Wis.	1880
Albuquerque, N. Mex.	1960
Syracuse, N.Y.	1900
Madison, Wis.	1970
Harrisburg, Pa.	1920[a]
Raleigh, N.C.	1970
Richmond, Va.	1910

[a]Census when the population exceeded 50,000.

masks an important difference: Houston, Columbus, Nashville, and Indianapolis passed the 100,000 population mark only a decade or two after the inelastic cities did; Albuquerque, Madison, and Raleigh are truly young cities.

What transformed the futures of Houston, Columbus, Nashville, and Indianapolis was, in large measure, the attitude of their community leadership (with citizen support). Houston and Columbus have been very expansionist through aggressive annexation (despite limitations on their legal powers). Even more striking, the leadership of Nashville and Indianapolis transformed their communities through successful city-county consolidations. Without city-county consolidation, which lifted both cities out of slow erosion, the current status of Nashville and Indianapolis would probably be not much different from that of Louisville and Milwaukee.

In short, on the eve of the suburban era, older, established cities tended to be complacent. Already centers of national or regional wealth, they focused on dividing up the pie rather than on making the pie larger. By 1950 the shift of people, jobs, and power to the suburbs was under way. A failure of initiative from within as well as legal, historical, and political constraints from without contributed to making many older cities inelastic.

By contrast, younger cities were cities "on the make" as they entered the postwar era. Certainly, many would benefit from macroeconomic changes (for example, the growth of industry in the Sunbelt). Many would even benefit from microeconomic changes in technology (for example, inexpensive air conditioning units for Sunbelt homes and offices). But many cities made their own futures through adopting expansive policies. They made their own "elasticity."

Lesson 14: Racial prejudice has shaped growth patterns.

Racial patterns helped set the stage for the different postwar growth patterns in different regions. The Northeast and Midwest had few Blacks and even fewer Hispanics in their small towns and rural areas; minorities were almost exclusively located in larger cities.[10] The South had significant numbers of Blacks in rural counties, and the West had numerous Hispanics in southwestern towns. The outward expansion of many southern and western cities would not cross a racial boundary as markedly as in the Northeast and Midwest, though in some southern communities the politics of White domination could put a special spin on annexation issues (see Box 1.3).

Admittedly, some factors in suburban growth in the early postwar decades were nonracial. Many middle-class families became suburbanites because the older cities lacked dream houses at affordable prices in good neighborhoods with good schools. Others went to the suburbs to flee high city taxes and low city politics or to live nearer new, suburban-based jobs.

Yet in many metro areas, racially motivated "White flight" was undeniably a major factor in suburban growth. "Good" neighborhoods with "good" schools often were seen as neighborhoods and schools without any Blacks and, to a lesser degree, without any Hispanics. After the civil rights revolution in the 1960s, neighborhoods and schools without *poor* Blacks and Hispanics met the "good" test.

Racial prejudice played a role in the evolution of overwhelmingly White suburbs surrounding increasingly Black cities. How strong a role is debatable, but the demographic, social, and economic consequences have become clear over the past forty years.

Lesson 15: Inelastic areas are more segregated than elastic areas.

Today the high concentration of Blacks and Hispanics, particularly poor Blacks and Hispanics, within central cities of inelastic areas dominates their social geography and the choices that middle-class families (White and Black) must make about where to live and work. Table 1.11 illustrates the measurable differences between inelastic areas and elastic areas in terms of residential segregation of Blacks. (For an explanation of the index used, see Box 1.4.)

As stated earlier, each pair in our sample has similar percentages of Blacks in the population metrowide. The sharply different metro growth patterns yielded sharply different racial populations for central cities.

TABLE 1.11
INELASTIC AREAS ARE MORE SEGREGATED THAN ELASTIC AREAS

Metro area	Percentage Black (1990)		Black segregation index
	Metro area	City	
Houston, Tex.	19%	27%	66
Detroit, Mich.	21	75	88
Columbus, Ohio	12	22	67
Cleveland, Ohio	19	46	85
Nashville, Tenn.	15	24	61
Louisville, Ky.	13	30	69
Indianapolis, Ind.	14	22	74
Milwaukee, Wis.	14	30	83
Albuquerque, N. Mex.	3	3	39
Syracuse, N.Y.	6	20	73
Madison, Wis.	3	4	48
Harrisburg, Pa.	7	50	76
Raleigh, N.C.	25	24	48
Richmond, Va.	29	55	59

Box 1.3 Annexation and the Federal Voting Rights Act

Since 1971, a new hurdle has existed for many municipalities' annexation powers—the federal Voting Rights Act.

Under section 5, municipalities in all or sections of 29 states with large Black, Hispanic, or Native American populations have been required to clear proposed annexations with the U.S. Department of Justice.

The federal concern has been that by annexing predominantly White outlying areas, municipalities would dilute the growing political strength of Blacks and Hispanics.

According to Justice Department sources, between 1971 and 1992, the Justice Department objected to 518 proposed annexations. To place this number in perspective, that was 1.5 percent of the 35,081 annexations submitted for review.[1]

Of these contested annexations, only 45—or 0.13 percent of the total—were ultimately prevented by either Justice Department objections or the federal courts. Many contested annexations were resolved by changes in the political system to enhance minority representation. Typically, such reforms involved shifting from at-large to districted local elections.

Perhaps the most famous and bitterly contested annexation was Richmond's annexation of 23 square miles of Chesterfield County in 1970. For seven years thereafter, federal courts blocked further city elections until the case was finally decided by the U.S. Supreme Court.[2]

Opponents charged that by annexing over 47,000 new residents (97 percent White), the White-dominated Richmond city council had sought to dilute growing Black political power.

Proponents argued that the annexation's purpose was to strengthen Richmond's middle-class population, acquire vacant land for residential, commercial, and industrial growth, and expand the tax base to meet Richmond's future revenue needs.

The irony is that both sides were correct. By unanimous vote, the U.S. Supreme Court ruled in 1975 that the annexation "was infected by the impermissible purpose of denying the right to vote based on race."[3] The Court allowed the annexation to stand, based on Richmond's shift to a nine-member council elected by wards.

Metro Houston is 19 percent black. Many of its new "suburbs" are within its city limits. The city of Houston is only 27 percent Black. Metro Detroit has a slightly higher Black population (21 percent) than does Houston's metro area. With all of its new sub-

After adding 47,000 new residents (and an estimated one-quarter to its tax base), the 1970 annexation, however, marked the end of Richmond's expansion. Blacks gained a majority of the ward council seats by 1978, electing Henry Marsh as Richmond's first Black mayor.

Richmond's Black community has gained political control of a depreciating asset. While the three adjacent counties have almost doubled with 221,000 new residents, Richmond's population has dropped by 46,000, or –19 percent since 1970. City income growth has steadily lagged behind suburban income growth. City incomes are now 83 percent of suburban incomes. Richmond's Black middle class is beginning to leave the city for suburban locations.

Richmond's annexation powers were effectively ended by the Virginia legislature, which in 1979 exempted urban counties from further annexation without county approval. Probably Richmond's Black majority city council would have lost all interest in further annexations in any event in order not to jeopardize its newly acquired political power.

The saga of Richmond's annexation battle epitomizes one of urban America's sad realities. In many cities, achieving political dominance has also trapped many Blacks or Hispanics in cities of declining social and economic opportunity. Minority political control seems to accelerate abandonment of the city by middle-class residents, investors, and employers.

1. These statistics are compiled by the author from a report entitled "Complete Listing of Objections Pursuant to the Voting Rights Act of 1965," issued by the Department of Justice, Voting Rights Division (December 31, 1992). I have treated one submission of 525 annexations by one South Carolina city in 1986 as a single submission. (The Justice Department's objection to that annexation package was ultimately withdrawn.)
2. All information on the history of the Richmond annexation dispute is taken from John V. Moeser and Rutledge M. Dennis, *The Politics of Annexation: Oligarchic Power in a Southern City* (Cambridge, Mass.: Schenkman Publishing Company, 1982).
3. Ibid., 172.

urbs outside its city limits, however, the city of Detroit is 75 percent Black.

The metrowide residential segregation index for Blacks in the Houston metro area is 66; for Blacks in the Detroit metro area it

---

Box 1.4 Census Bureau Calculates Residential Segregation

Building on the path-breaking work of sociologists Karl and Alma Taeuber, Douglas Massey, and Nancy Denton, the Census Bureau published a study of residential segregation in all 320 metro areas.[1] Using nineteen different statistical measures, the Census Bureau measured evenness, exposure, concentration, centralization, and clustering for Blacks, Hispanics, Asians, and American Indians. Calculations were conducted for all areas with Black, Hispanic, or Asian populations of 2 percent or more and of 1 percent or more American Indians.

Blacks are much more segregated than are Hispanics. Among large metro areas of 1 million or more people, the ten most segregated metro areas for Blacks are Detroit, Milwaukee, Cleveland, Newark, St. Louis, Chicago, Indianapolis, Philadelphia, New York, and Minneapolis-St. Paul. The least segregated large metro areas for Blacks are Middlesex-Somerset-Hunterdon, N.J., San Jose, Riverside-San Bernardino, Charlotte-Gastonia-Rock Hill, Norfolk-Virginia Beach-Newport News, San Diego, Phoenix, San Antonio, Nassau-Suffolk, Sacramento, and Seattle.

Throughout this book I have used the "Taeuber," or "dissimilarity index," as the sole measure of residential segregation. In effect, it measures "evenness"—what proportion of a minority population would have to move to produce an absolutely proportional distribution of that minority population across all census tracts of a metro area.

A dissimilarity index of 100 would indicate total segregation (that is, a completely uneven distribution of minorities); an index of 0 would indicate complete integration (that is, a completely even and uniform distribution of minorities).

1. Roderick J. Harrison and Daniel H. Weinberg, *Racial and Ethnic Segregation in 1990* (Washington, D.C.: U.S. Bureau of the Census, April 1992).

---

is 88. (Complete segregation equals 100; complete integration equals 0.)

Racial segregation in inelastic areas is consistently high. Segregation of Blacks is always less within the elastic metro area in a pair than it is in the inelastic metro area. Between metro areas in different regions (for example, Houston-Detroit, Albuquerque-Syracuse), differences in racial patterns might be explained in terms of broad regional differences (Sunbelt-Frostbelt, for example). The relationship, however, holds true between metro areas in the same region (Raleigh-Richmond, Nashville-Louisville) and even within the same state (Columbus-Cleveland).

Lesson 16: Inelastic areas that segregate Blacks segregate Hispanics.

Hispanics are significantly less segregated than are Blacks (although Hispanic segregation is growing in many areas). Typically, the level of Hispanic residential segregation is 20 to 30 points below Black segregation within the same metro area. In addition, southwestern communities tend to have many more Hispanics than do other areas of the country. In less elastic areas, however, even small Hispanic populations are usually highly segregated (Table 1.12).[11]

Lesson 17: City-suburb income gaps are more critical a problem than overall income levels in metro areas.

The city-suburb per capita income ratio is the single most important indicator of an urban area's social health (Table 1.13). Income levels in inelastic cities fall well below suburban levels (Detroit and Cleveland, 53 percent). Elastic cities, however, keep pace with suburban levels (Houston, 89 percent; Nashville, 98 percent) or even exceed suburban levels (Raleigh, 103 percent; Albuquerque, 118 percent).

The city-suburb per capita income ratio is also an almost unerring barometer of a mayor's national politics. In May 1992 many of the nation's mayors marched on the Congress and White House to appeal for $35 billion in new federal aid to urban areas. The mayors of Detroit, Cleveland, Louisville, Milwaukee, Syracuse, Harrisburg, and Richmond supported the "Save Our Cities" appeal. The mayors of elastic cities within our sample (with the exception of Madison's mayor) did not. Yet the metro areas from which the supportive mayors came had the same nominal income levels (an average $14,892 per capita) as did the metro areas of the nonsupportive mayors ($14,850)

The crux of the issue is the sharp disparities within the metro area. Inelastic cities had per capita incomes ($11,102) only 68 per-

TABLE 1.12
INELASTIC AREAS THAT SEGREGATE BLACKS
SEGREGATE HISPANICS

Metro area	Percentage Hispanic (1990)		Hispanic segregation index
	Metro area	City	
Houston, Tex.	21%	28%	49
Detroit, Mich.	2	3	(54)[a]
Columbus, Ohio	1	1	(32)
Cleveland, Ohio	2	5	(68)
Nashville, Tenn.	1	1	(42)
Louisville, Ky.	1	1	(34)
Indianapolis, Ind.	1	1	(43)
Milwaukee, Wis.	4	6	56
Albuquerque, N. Mex.	37	35	42
Syracuse, N.Y.	1	3	(47)
Madison, Wis.	2	2	(40)
Harrisburg, Pa.	2	8	(68)
Raleigh, N.C.	1	1	41
Richmond, Va.	1	1	N/A

[a]The Census Bureau study did not calculate indices of residential segregation of Hispanics in metro areas with less than a 2 percent Hispanic population. Because of the near identical relationship between Hispanic residential segregation and Hispanic school segregation, I have substituted Hispanic school segregation indices, where needed, from a study I conducted with the Urban Institute. These substitutions are indicated by parentheses.

cent of suburban levels, while income levels *within* elastic cities ($14,634) were equal (96 percent) to suburban levels. As a result, income levels for elastic cities were 32 percent above income levels of inelastic cities, even though both sets of cities are located in areas of nominally equal wealth.

Many mayors of inelastic cities go to Washington because they do not have the ability (or the inclination) to get their suburban neighbors to share the burden. They are trapped between having an ever smaller slice of the metro tax base and an ever growing share of metro social burdens.

Mayors of elastic cities, by contrast, find many of their "suburbs" within their own city limits. Their city revenue bases have expanded dramatically. Often city governments of elastic cities are better financed than are outlying jurisdictions. Poor minori-

TABLE 1.13
CITY-SUBURBAN INCOME GAPS ARE A MORE CRITICAL PROBLEM
THAN METRO INCOME LEVELS

| Metro area | Per capita income (1989) | | | City-suburb ratio |
	Metro area	City	Suburb	
Houston, Tex.	$15,091	$14,261	$16,012	89%
Detroit, Mich.	15,694	9,443	17,874	53
Columbus, Ohio	14,516	13,151	16,169	81
Cleveland, Ohio	15,092	9,258	17,317	53
Nashville, Tenn.	14,567	14,490	14,808	98
Louisville, Ky.	13,600	11,527	14,564	79
Indianapolis, Ind.	15,159	14,478	16,120	90
Milwaukee, Wis.	14,785	11,106	17,868	62
Albuquerque, N. Mex.	13,594	14,018	11,892	118
Syracuse, N.Y.	13,918	11,351	17,868	77
Madison, Wis.	15,542	15,143	15,976	95
Harrisburg, Pa.	14,659	11,037	15,251	72
Raleigh, N.C.	16,170	16,896	16,377	103
Richmond, Va.	15,848	13,993	16,777	83

ties are not heavily concentrated within the central city. For cities that are expanding very aggressively, the "suburbs" outside the city limits are often poor rural and semirural areas. Under such conditions mayors usually choose to handle local problems with local revenues rather than seek federal urban aid.

Lesson 18: Fragmented local government fosters segregation; unified local government promotes integration.

The fragmentation of metro areas into multiple local governments is associated with the degree of residential segregation.

For most Americans, smaller is better and home rule is an unassailable democratic good. But the sad reality is that the smaller the local jurisdiction or school district, the more narrow and exclusive the population served. In general, the more highly fragmented a metro area is, the more segregated it is racially and economically (Table 1.14). Smaller jurisdictions are typically organized to promote and protect uniformity rather than diversity. Conversely, areas characterized by geographically large, multi-powered governments and more unified school systems tend to promote more racial and economic integration and achieve greater social mobility.

The critical issue is the number of different governments that control planning and zoning decisions. The key measures are the proportion of the metro area under the central city's control (column one in Table 1.14) and the number of suburban jurisdictions with planning and zoning powers (column two in Table 1.14). The final two columns repeat the indices of residential segregation explained in Box 1.4.

The way a metro area is governed is not the only factor affecting integration. Another factor is age. Old cities generally have more decaying neighborhoods in which poor Blacks and Hispanics are concentrated. Younger cities have emerged in an era of somewhat more enlightened racial attitudes (and some effective civil rights laws). In addition, regional racial patterns and overall economic trends affect the degree of integration.

Does greater socioeconomic integration automatically flow from greater governmental unity? Probably not. What is clear is that, absent federal or state mandates, a metro area in which local government is highly fragmented is usually incapable of adopting broad, integrating strategies. Conversely, a metro area in which key planning and zoning powers are concentrated under a dominant local government has the potential to implement policies to promote greater racial and economic integration if that government has the courage and vision to do so.

Lesson 19: Dispersed and fragmented public education is more segregated than centralized and unified public education.

Table 1.15 depicts patterns in public education that parallel patterns in local general government. Public education in inelastic areas is characterized by a single, but shrinking, central-city school system surrounded by multiple suburban systems. Suburban Syracuse has 35 school systems; suburban Cleveland, 53; and suburban Detroit, 116!

By contrast, in elastic areas a unified, central-city school system is typically as dominant as the expanding central city. The

TABLE 1.14
FRAGMENTED LOCAL GOVERNMENT FOSTERS SEGREGATION;
UNIFIED LOCAL GOVERNMENT PROMOTES INTEGRATION

Metro area	Percentage of area population governed by central city	Number of suburban governments	Segregation index Blacks	Hispanics
Houston, Tex.	49%	79	66	49
Detroit, Mich.	23	338	88	(54)[a]
Columbus, Ohio	46	203	67	(32)
Cleveland, Ohio	28	62	85	(68)
Nashville, Tenn.	50	46	61	(42)
Louisville, Ky.	28	163	69	(34)
Indianapolis, Ind.	59	160	74	(43)
Milwaukee, Wis.	44	93	83	56
Albuquerque, N. Mex.	80	3	39	42
Syracuse, N.Y.	25	97	73	(47)
Madison, Wis.	52	59	48	(40)
Harrisburg, Pa.	9	132	76	(68)
Raleigh, N.C.	28	24	48	(41)
Richmond, Va.	23	18	59	N/A

[a]The Census Bureau study did not calculate indices of residential segregation of Hispanics in metro areas with less than a 2 percent Hispanic population. Because of the near identical relationship between Hispanic residential segregation and Hispanic school segregation, I have substituted Hispanic school segregation indices, where needed, from a study I conducted with the Urban Institute. These substitutions are indicated by parentheses.

Nashville public schools, for example, enroll 44 percent of metro area public school students.

Several Sunbelt states (for example, Florida and North Carolina) have countywide unified school districts that serve all or many of the municipalities within them. For instance, the four-county Raleigh-Durham area has twenty municipalities but only ten school districts. The Albuquerque public schools, the twenty-fifth largest system in the nation, serves not only all of Albuquerque and surrounding Bernalillo County but nearby communities in an adjacent county as well.

Table 1.15 measures school segregation metrowide by the same dissimilarity index I used to measure residential segregation

Box 1.5 School Segregation Parallels Residential Segregation, Except in South

School segregation closely tracks residential segregation, except in the South. With court-ordered desegregation plans in effect within typically large school systems, southern schools are more integrated than southern neighborhoods.

Prior to the Census Bureau study of residential segregation, the Urban Institute and I analyzed school segregation within all metro areas.

The basic data source for all researchers of residential segregation are annual reports submitted by the state education agencies to the U.S. Department of Education's National Center for Education Statistics. With funds from the National Urban League, my colleagues and I at the Urban Institute purchased computer tapes detailing public school districts and school enrollments by race and ethnicity for elementary and secondary schools for the 1989–90 school year.[1]

In analyzing school segregation I have used the same Taeuber, or dissimilarity index, used by the Census Bureau as one of the measures of residential segregation (see Box 1.4). The Census Bureau study analyzed the distribution of minority residents across all census tracts within each metro area. My study analyzed the distribution of minority students across all public high schools of all school districts within each metro area.

Of the largest metro areas of 1,000,000 or more residents, Black school segregation is highest in Detroit; Bergen-Passaic, New Jersey; Newark; Cleveland; Chicago; Cincinnati; Hartford; Philadelphia; Columbus, Ohio; and Milwaukee. The least segregated school systems for Blacks in large metro areas are Charlotte; Tampa-St. Petersburg-Clearwater; Anaheim-Santa Ana, California; Riverside-San Bernardino, California; San Jose; Orlando; San Antonio; Fort Lauderdale-Hollywood-Pompano Beach, Florida; Salt Lake City; and Middlesex-Somerset-Hunterdon, New Jersey.

---

1. The data were incomplete, however. Eight states annually did not submitted information: Georgia, Idaho, Maine, Missouri, Montana, South Dakota, Virginia, and Wyoming. Among metro areas of 1,000,000 or more people, missing state reports prevented analysis of Washington, D.C.-Maryland-Virginia; Atlanta, Georgia; Kansas City, Missouri-Kansas; and St. Louis, Missouri-Illinois.

Table 1.15

Dispersed and Fragmented Public Education Is More
Segregated than Centralized and Unified
Public Education

Metro area	Percentage of metro area students enrolled in city schools	Number of suburban school districts	School segregation index	
			Blacks	Hispanics
Houston, Tex.	29%	38	59	50
Detroit, Mich.	23	116	90	54
Columbus, Ohio	25	52	71	32
Cleveland, Ohio	24	53	79	68
Nashville, Tenn.	41	7	47	42
Louisville, Ky.	64	9	37	34
Indianapolis, Ind.	19	44	62	43
Milwaukee, Wis.	38	36	70	58
Albuquerque, N. Mex.	100	0	31	44
Syracuse, N.Y.	15	35	76	47
Madison, Wis.	44	15	51	40
Harrisburg, Pa.	9	23	82	68
Raleigh, N.C.	57	10	32	41
Richmond, Va.	15	12	N/A	N/A

metrowide. (See Box 1.4 for an explanation of this index.) Elastic areas are much less segregated for Black students (50) than are inelastic areas (72). Despite typically much larger Hispanic populations in elastic areas, the pattern of lower segregation holds for Hispanic students in elastic areas (42) as compared with inelastic areas (60).

Skeptics may argue that most southern school systems have federal court-ordered desegregation plans in effect. This is quite true, but because these systems are often countywide, they typically link city and suburb. Middle-class Whites cannot flee to other public school systems. Desegregation in these areas has been more successful and more stable than in areas where school desegregation plans apply solely within a central-city school system. Such limited school desegregation efforts have often prompted White flight to private schools or suburban systems.

The biggest departure from the pattern of elastic-inelastic communities in Table 1.15 (Louisville) illustrates these observations. In 1975, by federal court order, the city of Louisville's school system was merged with the Jefferson County school system to create one countywide school system. Within this unified system an aggressive and successful program of both racial integration and school reform has been under way for twenty years. A high degree of racial integration in the schools (37 for Blacks) and limited White flight from the system have been the result. Although the city of Louisville's population has dropped precipitously, the population of the rest of Jefferson County outside Louisville has increased 20 percent since the school system merger.

Tables 1.14 and 1.15 show that for Blacks, elastic-area schools are more desegregated (50) than are elastic-area neighborhoods (58). In highly fragmented, inelastic metro areas, Black school segregation (79) almost perfectly mirrors Black neighborhood segregation (81).

Especially when buttressed by federal court orders, broad-based public school systems are integrating mechanisms for elastic areas, while fragmented school structures (which frustrate desegregation efforts) reinforce racial segregation in inelastic areas.

These patterns of local governance suggest a second law of urban dynamics: *fragmentation divides; unification unites.* This second law is subject, perhaps, to greater "relativity." Anecdotal proof is easier to compile than constructing compelling statistical proof.

Lesson 20: The global economy sets the rules, but local areas can decide how to play the game.

I certainly would not argue that major economic changes are driven by urban development patterns. The "deindustrialization" of the American economy, for example, is the result primarily of global competition in manufacturing in recent decades, not the ways in which metro areas have developed.

Deindustrialization has affected urban areas very differently. Table 1.16 shows these effects during the 1973–88 period (when deindustrialization was already well advanced).

The inelastic cities reached maturity during the industrial age. Their metro areas in 1973 were more highly industrialized (25 percent) than were elastic metro areas (16 percent). Moreover, their industrial bases (particularly Detroit's, Cleveland's, and Milwaukee's) emphasized "smokestack industries"—steel, automobiles, and other metal trades. These industries were among those hardest hit by international competition. The loss of manufacturing jobs was catastrophic for Detroit, Cleveland, Louisville, and Milwaukee. Inelastic areas, however, did gain in overall employment (23 percent), although manufacturing employment dropped from 25 percent to 17 percent of all jobs.

Several elastic areas (Albuquerque, Madison, Raleigh) grew up largely during the postindustrial era. New products such as computers and electronic components often characterized these metro areas' industrial activities. Albuquerque, Madison, and Raleigh built impressively on small manufacturing bases. Yet, except for Madison, manufacturing declined in importance in each of these elastic areas.

To test my thesis about elastic versus inelastic cities, it is best to examine metro areas within the same region or state. This

TABLE 1.16

ELASTIC AREAS ADJUST BETTER TO ECONOMIC CHANGE
THAN INELASTIC AREAS

Metro area	Percentage of metro jobs in manufacturing		Percent change in manufacturing jobs
	1973	1988	1973–88
Houston, Tex.	15%	10%	3%
Detroit, Mich.	32	21	−25
Columbus, Ohio	21	13	−14
Cleveland, Ohio	30	20	−29
Nashville, Tenn.	21	15	9
Louisville, Ky.	27	17	−26
Indianapolis, Ind.	23	15	−16
Milwaukee, Wis.	30	21	−17
Albuquerque, N. Mex.	9	7	51
Syracuse, N.Y.	22	15	−12
Madison, Wis.	10	10	48
Harrisburg, Pa.	21	15	−8
Raleigh, N.C.	15	13	58
Richmond, Va.	18	12	−5

minimizes Sunbelt-Frostbelt confusion. For example, while inelastic Louisville lost industrial jobs (–26 percent), elastic Nashville gained (+9 percent); while inelastic Richmond lost industrial jobs (–5 percent), elastic Raleigh gained (+58 percent).

More striking are the contrasts between areas that have both been caught up by deindustrialization. Both Columbus and Cleveland lost many manufacturing jobs, but elastic Columbus boomed while inelastic Cleveland stagnated. The percentage decline in manufacturing jobs was about the same in elastic Indianapolis and inelastic Milwaukee, but Indianapolis is clearly the more economically vigorous area.

Past prosperity may have lulled old industrial areas into complacency. Many have failed to tool up for economic change. The level of education of the labor force is a good measure of adaptability of areas to the postindustrial, information age. As shown in Table 1.17, the elastic areas boast higher percentages of workers with B.A. degrees or above (25 percent) than the inelastic areas (20 percent).[12]

Lesson 21: The smaller the income gap between city and suburb, the greater the economic progress for the whole metropolitan community.

The National League of Cities has released a widely reported study that concluded that, of forty-eight large metro areas, those with the smallest central city/suburban income gaps had the greatest job increases.[13]

Table 1.18 tests this observation for the pairs of metro areas. For inelastic areas the city-suburb income ratio was 68 percent; from 1973 to 1988 the overall growth in jobs was 23 percent. By contrast, in elastic areas (with a city-suburb income ratio of 96 percent) the fifteen-year growth in employment was 58 percent.

Job growth can be just a proxy for population growth. Are the lives of elastic area residents getting better compared with those of inelastic area residents? The answer is yes, although not as dramatically as the differential in employment growth. From 1969 to 1989, real per capita income in these elastic areas grew 41 percent compared with 30 percent in inelastic areas (Table 1.19). This growth occurred despite the decade-long collapse in oil and gas and real estate prices in the Southwest that severely depressed income growth in Houston and Albuquerque.

TABLE 1.17

ELASTIC AREAS TEND TO HAVE A HIGHER EDUCATED WORK FORCE THAN INELASTIC AREAS

Metro area	Percentage of metro area workers with B.A. degrees or above, 1990
Houston, Tex.	25%
Detroit, Mich.	18
Columbus, Ohio	23
Cleveland, Ohio	20
Nashville, Tenn.	21
Louisville, Ky.	17
Indianapolis, Ind.	21
Milwaukee, Wis.	21
Albuquerque, N. Mex.	27
Syracuse, N.Y.	22
Madison, Wis.	34
Harrisburg, Pa.	18
Raleigh, N.C.	25
Richmond, Va.	24

These observations lead to my third law of urban dynamics: *ties do bind.* Admittedly, the data are mixed. If this were a physics text, the third law might be described as a weak nuclear force. Can suburbs successfully create viable, self-contained suburban economies and abandon their central cities? Can America *afford* to bet on the answer?

Lesson 22: Poverty is more concentrated in inelastic cities than in elastic cities.

What about poverty levels? Historically, the South and West have been lower income regions than the Northeast and Midwest. That pattern still persists (Table 1.20). A slightly higher percentage of the population fell below the poverty line in southern and western areas (12 percent) than in northeastern and midwestern areas (10 percent), regardless of local metropolitan dynamics. However, poverty is much more concentrated in the inelastic cities (25 percent) than in the elastic cities (15 percent).

TABLE 1.18
ELASTIC AREAS HAVE FASTER RATES OF JOB CREATION THAN
INELASTIC AREAS

Metro area	City-suburb per capita income rate ratio 1989	Metro job growth 1973–88
Houston, Tex.	89%	67%
Detroit, Mich.	53	11
Columbus, Ohio	81	40
Cleveland, Ohio	53	8
Nashville, Tenn.	98	55
Louisville, Ky.	79	21
Indianapolis, Ind.	90	34
Milwaukee, Wis.	62	22
Albuquerque, N. Mex.	118	75
Syracuse, N.Y.	77	27
Madison, Wis.	95	51
Harrisburg, Pa.	72	29
Raleigh, N.C.	103	81
Richmond, Va.	83	46

In part, the pattern is regional. In the South and West, many poor households still live in rural and semiurban sections of the metro areas. Poverty is both more spread out in the countryside and more dispersed within the urbanized area itself. But concentrated poverty is also the result of cities' inelasticity, which magnifies economic segregation.

A simple measure of disproportionate concentration of poverty in a central city is what I have called a city's "fair share of poverty index." The index is the ratio between the city's percentage of poor residents and the total metro area's percentage of poor residents. Elastic cities are home to only slightly more than their fair share of the metro area poor (index: 128). By contrast, inelastic cities must cope with too many poor people (index: 234).

As social tinder, poverty in elastic areas typically lacks the critical mass it has in the highly concentrated ghettos of inelastic cities of the Northeast and Midwest.

TABLE 1.19
ELASTIC AREAS SHOW GREATER GAINS IN REAL INCOME THAN
INELASTIC AREAS

Metro area	Percentage growth in real per capita income in metro areas, 1969–89
Houston, Tex.	36%
Detroit, Mich.	26
Columbus, Ohio	34
Cleveland, Ohio	23
Nashville, Tenn.	49
Louisville, Ky.	30
Indianapolis, Ind.	32
Milwaukee, Wis.	25
Albuquerque, N. Mex.	41
Syracuse, N.Y.	29
Madison, Wis.	34
Harrisburg, Pa.	33
Raleigh, N.C.	62
Richmond, Va.	45

Lesson 23: Elastic cities have better bond ratings than inelastic cities.

City-suburb income disparities are further reflected in municipal bond markets. Bond rating agencies must assess the risk associated with a city government's debts. Ratings are based on long-term economic outlook and past debt management. The highest rating (AAA) indicates a blue-chip investment. A rating of BA or lower indicates a "junk bond," which typically cannot be purchased by pension funds and other institutional investors.

The debt management of some inelastic cities (Milwaukee, Syracuse, Richmond) has been better than their social management (Table 1.21), but the patterns for elastic and inelastic cities hold. The elastic cities averaged AA1 ratings. Inelastic cities averaged A1 ratings. Detroit and Harrisburg are in severe fiscal distress.

Finally, what is statistically clear if politically unacknowledged is the last lesson that I draw from these past forty years of urban America.

Table 1.20

Poverty Is More Concentrated in Inelastic Cities than in Elastic Cities

Metro area	Percentage of metro population below the poverty line, 1990	Percentage of city population below the poverty line, 1990	City's fair share index of metro area poor population, 1990
Houston, Tex.	15%	21%	137
Detroit, Mich.	13	32	251
Columbus, Ohio	12	17	146
Cleveland, Ohio	12	29	243
Nashville, Tenn.	11	13	119
Louisville, Ky.	13	23	178
Indianapolis, Ind.	10	12	130
Milwaukee, Wis.	12	22	191
Albuquerque, N. Mex.	15	14	96
Syracuse, N.Y.	10	23	218
Madison, Wis.	10	16	153
Harrisburg, Pa.	8	27	346
Raleigh, N.C.	10	12	116
Richmond, Va.	10	21	213

Lesson 24: Rebuilding inner cities from within has not happened.

After the 1992 riot in South Central Los Angeles, the most ominous news story I read detailed not what had just happened in South Central Los Angeles but what had not happened in the Watts section of Los Angeles in the twenty-seven years since the rioting there in 1965. Public and private efforts in Watts had not overcome continued economic and social decay. Indeed, successful clients of job training and other social programs moved out of Watts to better communities elsewhere in the Los Angeles area—a rational decision on their part.

It does not take riots to push inelastic cities into accelerated decline, although riots hasten the process. A combination of sustained population loss (20 percent or more), a disproportionately high minority population (typically, 30 percent or more), and a

TABLE 1.21
ELASTIC CITIES HAVE BETTER BOND RATINGS THAN
INELASTIC CITIES

Metro area	City bond rating
Houston, Tex.	AA
Detroit, Mich.	BA1
Columbus, Ohio	AA1
Cleveland, Ohio	A
Nashville, Tenn.	AA
Louisville, Ky.	A1
Indianapolis, Ind.	AAA
Milwaukee, Wis.	AA1
Albuquerque, N. Mex.	AA
Syracuse, N.Y.	AA
Madison, Wis.	AAA
Harrisburg, Pa.	BAA
Raleigh, N.C.	AAA
Richmond, Va.	A1

significant city-suburb income gap (70 percent or less) seems to define the point of no return for a central city.

Table 1.22 details the status of our paired cities regarding these three preconditions as of about 1980. The table also presents what has happened to the overall city population, percentage of minorities, and city-suburb income ratio in the decade since.

As a group the elastic cities continued to grow in population and basically maintained their parity in city-suburb income ratio, while increasing only slightly the percentage of minorities (from 31 percent to 32 percent). Inelastic cities, however, continued to slide downward on all counts. During the decade, the overall population fell further from earlier peaks, the city-suburb income gap widened (from 79 percent to 69 percent), and the minority population increased from 46 percent to 49 percent— almost three times the rate of increase of the elastic cities.

Of our sample inelastic cities only Detroit and Cleveland had dropped below all three critical levels, although all the others

TABLE 1.22

In Inelastic Cities, the Population Continues to Decline, the Minority Ratio Continues to Increase, and the City-Suburb Income Gap Continues to Widen

Metro area	Change in city population*		Percentage of minorities in city		City-suburb income ratio	
	By 1980	By 1990	1980	1990	1979	1989
Houston, Tex.	171%	174%	52%	58%	95%	89%
Detroit, Mich.	-35	-44	71	79	66	53
Columbus, Ohio	50	68	25	25	85	81
Cleveland, Ohio	-37	-45	50	53	63	53
Nashville, Tenn.	161	180	26	27	102	98
Louisville, Ky.	-19	-31	30	31	84	79
Indianapolis, Ind.	64	71	24	24	95	90
Milwaukee, Wis.	0	-15	36	39	82	62
Albuquerque, N. Mex.	244	297	41	42	124	118
Syracuse, N.Y.	-23	-26	24	26	87	77
Madison, Wis.	92	99	10	10	98	95
Harrisburg, Pa.	-41	-42	55	59	82	72
Raleigh, N.C.	139	217	38	39	102	103
Richmond, Va.	-5	-19	54	57	90	85

*Population changes are measured either from 1950 or a city's peak population after 1950.

were moving in that direction. This inexorable downward trend of inelastic cities suggests the fourth law of urban dynamics: *ghettos can only become bigger ghettos.*

Conclusion

Looking back over all the lessons learned, what composite profile can be drawn for inelastic and elastic areas?

An inelastic area has a central city frozen within its city limits and surrounded by growing suburbs. It may have a strong downtown business district as a regional employment center, but its city neighborhoods are increasingly catch basins for poor Blacks and Hispanics. With the flight of middle-class families, the city's population has dropped steadily (typically by 20 percent or more). The income gap between city residents and suburbanites steadily widens. City government is squeezed between rising service needs and eroding incomes. Unable to tap the areas of greater economic growth (its suburbs), the city becomes increasingly reliant on federal and state aid. The suburbs are typically fragmented into multiple towns and small cities and mini school systems. This very fragmentation of local government reinforces racial and economic segregation. Rivalry among jurisdictions often inhibits the whole area's ability to respond to economic challenges.

In an elastic area suburban subdivisions expand around the central city, but the central city is able to expand as well and capture much of that suburban growth within its municipal boundaries. Although no community is free of racial inequities, minorities are more evenly spread throughout the area. Segregation by race and income class is reduced. City incomes are typically equal to or higher than suburban incomes. Tapping a broader tax base, an elastic city government is better financed and more inclined to rely on local resources to address local problems. In fact, local public institutions, in general, tend to be more unified and promote more united and effective responses to economic challenges.

Notes

1. The 1950 census did not identify Hispanics as either a racial or ethnic group (aside from about 600,000 foreign-born Hispanics of Mexican and other Latin American origin). I have adopted an estimate of about 4 million Hispanics in 1950.

2. A majority of all Blacks live in metropolitan New York, Chicago, Los Angeles, Philadelphia, Detroit, Atlanta, Houston, Baltimore, Miami, Dallas-Fort Worth, San Francisco, Oakland, Cleveland, New Orleans, St. Louis, Memphis, Norfolk-Virginia Beach-Newport News, Richmond-Petersburg, Birmingham, Charlotte, Milwaukee, Cincinnati, Kansas City, Tampa-St. Petersburg-Clearwater, and Washington, D.C. Adding San Antonio, San Diego, El Paso, and San Jose to these metro areas accounts for a majority of all Hispanics. Adding Honolulu covers a majority of all Asians.

3. In 1790 the national population density was 4.5 persons per square mile. In 1990 for a country four times as large in area (including Alaska), the national population density was 70.3 persons per square mile.

4. For the 193 central cities identified as such in the 1950 census, the average density was 7,517 persons per square mile.

5. I do not mean "upward" literally—that is, through high-rise development—but through low-density, in-fill development. A low-density city's population density, in effect, can move upward.

6. The designation of "elastic" or "inelastic" is always based on the characteristics of a central city. Although a metro area also will be referred to as an elastic area or inelastic area, that qualifier reflects its central city's status.

7. Among 320 metro areas the only exceptions are New York City, Pittsburgh, Jersey City, St. Joseph (Missouri), and eight mining industry regions.

8. Examples are Baltimore, Philadelphia, San Francisco, and St. Louis. Virginia's "independent cities" had strong annexation powers until 1979 when the legislature placed, in effect, a moratorium on further annexation.

9. In Table 1.9, Davidson and Marion counties' negative growth "outside the city" reflects the incorporation of existing residents into the new consolidated governments of Nashville-Davidson and Indianapolis-Marion County.

10. Until ratification of the Fourteenth Amendment to the U.S. Constitution in 1868, some northeastern and midwestern states had Black exclusion laws. One example is Indiana.

12. Indeed, the presence of a major, high-quality university is often an engine supporting local, postindustrial growth. Between our two sample groups the major universities in elastic areas are Houston-Rice, Ohio State, Vanderbilt, Indiana (Indianapolis campus), New Mexico, Wisconsin, and the Research Triangle's Duke-North Carolina-North Carolina State. Major universities in inelastic areas are Wayne State, Cleveland State-Case Western Reserve, Louisville, Marquette-Wisconsin (Milwaukee campus), Syracuse, Dickinson College, and Virginia Commonwealth-Richmond.

13. William R. Barnes and Larry C. Ledebur. *City Distress, Metropolitan Disparities, and Economic Growth.* Washington, D.C., National League of Cities, September 1992.

Chapter II

Characteristics of Metropolitan Areas

How does this concept of city elasticity affect demographic, social, and economic patterns of all cities and metro areas beyond the fourteen examined in Chapter I? To analyze this phenomenon I have constructed an "elasticity score" for the 522 central cities in the nation's 320 Metropolitan Statistical Areas.

The 320 metro areas in America range in population from Los Angeles (8,863,164) to Enid, Oklahoma (56,735). Lumping areas of such disparate size into common categories produces "averages" that hide more than they reveal. Therefore, I will exclude from further discussion the lowest end of the scale—the 131 metro areas with fewer than 200,000 residents in 1990.[1] Of the 189 remaining metro areas, four other groups seem to march to a different drummer. For the following reasons these also are being excluded from my proposed categories.

First, I exclude three "Mexican border towns": El Paso, McAllen-Edinburg-Mission, and Brownsville-Harlingen. Along with Laredo, a smaller metro area, these Texas communities sit on the northern bank of the Rio Grande opposite major Mexican communities. With high resident populations of Hispanics (70 percent to 94 percent) and thousands of Mexican workers and shoppers commuting daily across the border, these Texas cities are really economic and sociological extensions of northern Mexico.

Second, I exclude five "declining mining regions," along with six smaller mining areas. These regions have lost population and wealth because of the decades-long decline of coal mining in West Virginia and Appalachian Pennsylvania, Ohio, and Maryland, and of iron ore mining around Duluth, Minnesota, and Superior, Wisconsin. Their central cities have lost population and wealth as well.[2]

Third, I exclude from further analysis thirteen "White-only metro areas." These thirteen areas have few Blacks (0.9 percent) and few Hispanics (2.4 percent). Their small Black and Hispanic communities seem to be exposed "only" to minimal-to-moderate levels of residential and school segregation. Once again, including these areas in the larger analysis would distort the averages of the categories.[3]

The last group—"city-less metro areas"—is set apart for a purely technical reason. This group is composed of the three larger metro areas that the federal government has designated without central cities within their boundaries. To these three I have added two smaller, city-less metro areas. All are subunits of Consolidated Metropolitan Statistical Areas (CMSAs). They are Brazoria County, Texas (greater Houston); Beaver County, Pennsylvania (greater Pittsburgh); and Nassau-Suffolk counties, New York; Orange County, New York; and Monmouth-Ocean Counties, New Jersey (all in greater New York). Within these areas, employment locations are highly dispersed; their real central cities, of course, are Houston, Pittsburgh, and New York City.

After excluding all of the above, I have 165 metro areas for further categorization. The range of characteristics is still wide: in metro population, from Los Angeles (8,863,164) to Gainesville, Florida (204,111); in municipal area, from Anchorage, Alaska, (1,698 square miles) to York, Pennsylvania (5 square miles); in nominal metro per capita income, from Fairfield County, Connecticut ($26,161) to Visalia-Tulare-Porterville, California ($9,318); in Black population metrowide, from Jackson, Mississippi (42 percent) to Boulder-Longmont, Colorado (0.8 percent); in Hispanic population metrowide, from Corpus Christi, Texas (52 percent) to Birmingham, Alabama (0.4 percent).

To cut down the variation, I have separated metro areas with principal central cities under 100,000 population from metro areas with principal central cities over 100,000 population. In trying to classify all these areas coherently, I have not excluded any from my initial analysis. I have applied the same elasticity criteria to all 320 metro areas and 522 central cities.

Among the 117 major metro areas with principal central cities above 100,000 population, the range of characteristics is still wide. Therefore, a lot of emphasis should not be placed by readers on summarizing the characteristics of different categories. The most telling tests of my point of view—the effects of urban elasticity and inelasticity—are comparisons of cities within the same region, state, or even metro area.

TABLE 2.1
SUMMARY OF CATEGORIES

Category	Large metro areas	Small metro areas	Total metro areas
Mexican border towns	3	1	4
Declining mining regions	5	6	11
White-only metro areas	13	0	13
City-less metro areas	3	2	5
Large central cities (100,000+ residents)	117	0	117
Smaller central cities (fewer than 100,000 residents)	48	0	48
Smallest central cities and metro areas	0	122	122
TOTAL	189	131	320

The results are summarized in Table 2.1. All 522 central cities are categorized by relative elasticity in Appendix A. The elasticity score represents the combined effect of a city's density (population per square mile) in 1950 and the degree to which it expanded its city limits between 1950 and 1990. Each city's initial density and degree of boundary expansion (by percentage) are ranked against those of all other cities in its group. A city's relative rankings (organized by decile) for the two key characteristics (initial density and boundary expansion) are added together to produce a composite elasticity score with the degree of boundary expansion awarded three times the weight of initial density.

New York City ranks in the lowest decile (1) for having one of the highest population densities in 1950 (25,046 per square mile). It also ranks in the lowest decile (1) for not expanding its city limits at all. Therefore, New York City's elasticity score is 4 $(1 + 3 \times 1)$. Anchorage, Alaska, ranks in the next to highest decile (9) for having among the lowest population densities in 1950 (3,539 per square mile). It ranks in the highest decile (10) for having one of the highest boundary expansion rates (13,482 percent). Therefore, Anchorage's elasticity score is an almost perfect 39 $(9 + 3 \times 10)$.[4]

I have ranked all cities by their elasticity scores into deciles and split them into five groupings: zero elasticity, low elasticity, medium elasticity, high elasticity, and hyper elasticity. (New

---

Box 2.1 Whatever Happened to the City of Spring Garden?

What ever happened to Spring Garden, Northern Liberties, Kensington, Southwark, and Moyamensing? In 1850 these Pennsylvania communities were the ninth, eleventh, twelfth, twentieth, and twenty-eighth most populous cities in America! Four years later they were annexed to the larger city of Philadelphia to frame the boundaries of Philadelphia substantially as we know it today.

In fact, ten of the country's fifty largest cities in 1850 disappeared before 1900. They all were consolidated into larger governmental bodies.

In 1867 Boston annexed the city of Roxbury; seven years later it leaped across Boston Harbor to annex the city of Charlestown. Allegheny in 1907 was taken in by Pittsburgh. And in the tradition of "little fish-big fish-bigger fish," the twenty-fourth largest city in 1850, Williamsburgh, was annexed in 1854 by the city of Brooklyn (seventh largest), which in turn became part of New York City in 1898 (see Box 1.2).

The political geography of mature metropolitan areas may appear immutable to their residents today, but a century ago compelling public interests were served by such consolidations. Popular opposition as well as natural obstacles (harbors and rivers) had to be overcome, but the effort was worthwhile. These new governmental structures served their communities well for many decades.

York City is at the bottom of the zero-elasticity group; Anchorage leads the hyper-elasticity group.) The 117 largest areas are ranked in ascending order of elasticity (Table 2.2).[5]

The twenty-three-member zero-elasticity group includes three inelastic cities analyzed in Chapter I (Detroit, Cleveland, and Syracuse). This group also includes New York, Chicago, St. Louis, Pittsburgh, Newark, Philadelphia, Baltimore, and Washington, D.C.—regular tenants of most lists of troubled cities. In addition, the zero-elasticity group includes Boston, San Francisco, and Minneapolis—cities conventionally viewed as being in relatively good shape.

The twenty-two-member low-elasticity group includes Louisville, Milwaukee, and Richmond (discussed in Chapter I) as well as Los Angeles, Seattle, Norfolk, New Orleans, Honolulu, Miami, Portland, and Oakland. It may be surprising to find Los

TABLE 2.2

117 MAJOR METRO AREAS GROUPED BY RELATIVE ELASTICITY

Zero Elasticity	Low Elasticity	Medium Elasticity	High Elasticity	Hyper Elasticity
New York, N.Y.	Springfield, Mass.	Evansville, Ind.	Albuquerque*, N. Mex.	Vallejo*, Calif.
Newark, N.J.	Worcester, Mass.	Des Moines, Iowa	Sacramento, Calif.	Little Rock, Ark.
Paterson, N.J.	Los Angeles, Calif.	Birmingham, Ala.	Fort Worth, Tex.	Lexington, Ky.
Boston, Mass.	Oakland, Calif.	Gary*, Ind.	Columbus, Ohio	Tulsa, Okla.
St. Louis, Mo.	Miami, Fla.	Toledo, Ohio	Madison, Wisc.	Tampa, Fla.
Providence, R.I.	Tacoma, Wash.	Omaha, Nebr.	Santa Rosa*, Calif.	Montgomery, Ala.
Detroit, Mich.	New Orleans, La.	Peoria, Ill.	Dallas, Tex.	Orlando*, Fla.
Washington, D.C.	Honolulu*, Hawaii	Denver, Colo.	Modesto*, Calif.	Fresno, Calif.
Pittsburgh, Pa.	Allentown, Pa.	Lansing, Mich.	Kansas City, Mo.	Raleigh*, N.C.
Cleveland, Ohio	Albany, N.Y.	Anaheim*, Calif.	Macon, Ga.	Greensboro, N.C.
Baltimore, Md.	Milwaukee, Wisc.	Fort Wayne, Ind.	Shreveport, La.	Nashville, Tenn.
Hartford, Conn.	Seattle, Wash.	Ann Arbor*, Mich.	Chattanooga, Tenn.	Columbus, Ga.
Minneapolis, Minn.	Flint, Mich.	Fort Lauderdale*, Fla.	Las Vegas*, Nev.	Jacksonville, Fla.
Rochester, N.Y.	Grand Rapids, Mich.	Rockford, Ill.	Wichita, Kans.	Lubbock*, Tex.
Syracuse, N.Y.	Erie, Pa.	Salinas*, Calif.	San Diego, Calif.	Corpus Christi, Tex.
Jersey City, N.J.	South Bend, Ind.	Lincoln, Nebr.	Mobile, Ala.	Oklahoma City, Okla.
New Haven, Conn.	Louisville, Ky.	Riverside, Calif.	Huntsville*, Ala.	Phoenix, Ariz.
Chicago, Ill.	Richmond, Va.	Memphis, Tenn.	Charlotte, N.C.	Colorado Springs*, Colo.
San Francisco, Calif.	Norfolk, Va.	Savannah, Ga.	San Antonio, Tex.	Austin, Tex.
Philadelphia, Pa.	Portland, Oreg.	Baton Rouge*, La.	Stockton, Calif.	San Jose, Calif.
Buffalo, N.Y.	Akron, Ohio	Oxnard*, Calif.	Houston, Tex.	Reno*, Nev.
Bridgeport, Conn.	Dayton, Ohio	Atlanta, Ga.	Jackson, Miss.	Bakersfield*, Calif.
Cincinnati, Ohio		Beaumont, Tex.	Indianapolis, Ind.	Tucson*, Ariz.
		Knoxville, Tenn.		Tallahassee*, Fla.
				Anchorage*, Alaska

An asterisk (*) indicates that the city was not identified as a central city in the 1950 census.

Box 2.2 Hartford and Saginaw: Elasticity within Metro Areas

Within the same metro areas, the elasticity of cities differs. Elasticity helps determine the demographic, economic, and social characteristics of a city's future. Let us look within two metro areas: Hartford and Saginaw-Bay City-Midland.

Over the past forty years the Hartford metro area's population grew 72 percent. It is nominally the country's thirteenth most prosperous metro area, and it has a relatively small Black population metrowide (8 percent). City elasticities are strictly a function of the level of prior development. Political boundaries are fixed. In 1950 Hartford was a high-density city; New Britain, average density; and Middletown and Bristol, low density.

City	City elasticity score	City population 1950–90	City-suburb income ratio	City percentage Black
Hartford	*5	–21%	53%	36%
New Britain	6	2	70	7
Bristol	12	69	81	2
Middletown	13	44	85	11

*The elasticity for this city was scored within the group of larger cities (100,000 or more residents). The elasticity for the other cities in the table was scored among the smaller cities (fewer than 100,000 residents) for major metro areas.

Angeles among the low-elasticity group. However, low-density Los Angeles annexed vast areas in the 1920s and 1930s. Relying on extensive in-fill development, Los Angeles has expanded its city limits very little since 1950.

Of the cities analyzed in Chapter I, Denver, Atlanta, and Memphis are among the twenty-four medium-elasticity cities. Albuquerque, Columbus, Madison, Houston and Indianapolis-Marion (discussed in Chapter I) are among the twenty-three high-elasticity cities as well as Sacramento, Kansas City, Dallas and Forth Worth, San Diego, San Antonio, and Charlotte.

The twenty-five hyper-elasticity cities include Raleigh and Nashville-Davidson, both analyzed in Chapter I, along with other city-county consolidations, such as Lexington-Fayette, Columbus-Muskogee, Jacksonville-Duval, and Anchorage-Anchorage Borough. (Indianapolis-Marion just missed out.) The list of hyper-elasticity cities is rounded out by such annexation

The Saginaw-Bay City-Midland, Michigan, area shows how cities can make fateful choices. In the 1950's Saginaw and Midland jointly built a major water pipeline from Lake Huron. Saginaw sold city water to new subdivisions in neighboring townships. By contrast, Midland's policy was "no water without annexation." As a result, Saginaw remained locked within its boundaries, while Midland grew from 6 to 28 square miles. Forty years later Midland is probably Michigan's most successful central city, while Saginaw is one of the state's most distressed.

City	City elasticity score	City population 1950–90	City-suburb income ratio	City percentage Black
Saginaw	6	−25%	66%	40%
Bay City	6	−24	79	3
Midland	28	66	142	2

The patterns noted between elastic and inelastic cities at regional and state levels hold within the same metro areas. Inelastic cities lose population, develop sharp income gaps between city and suburb, and become more minority. Elastic cities gain population, generally maintain better income position, and tend to concentrate minorities less.

powerhouses as Phoenix, Austin, San Jose, Oklahoma City, and Tucson.

A similar analysis has been applied to the 48 metro areas with principal central cities under 100,000 (Harrisburg is a zero-elasticity member of this category) as well as to the 131 smaller metro areas.

Table 2.3 summarizes the average population growth of the metro areas in each group. The zero-elasticity group began and ended with the largest average metro population and experienced the lowest rate of metro population growth (30 percent).[6] The other groups doubled or tripled their populations. Disparities in growth *rates*, however important, should not be allowed to obscure the fact that all groups, including the zero-elasticity group, added an average of 500,000 to 650,000 residents between 1950 and 1990.

Table 2.4 demonstrates the dramatically different picture

TABLE 2.3
ALMOST ALL METRO AREAS HAVE GROWN

Metro Area	Average metro population		Percentage change 1950–90
	1950	1990	
Zero-Elasticity	1,862,390	2,424,192	30%
Low-Elasticity	699,864	1,342,168	92
Medium-Elasticity	319,449	824,470	158
High-Elasticity	384,898	1,012,949	163
Hyper-Elasticity	242,812	727,576	200

among central cities. The twenty-three zero-elasticity cities all lost population (an average of –23 percent) except for Paterson, New Jersey, which gained a marginal 1 percent because heavy Hispanic immigration offset other population loss.

Although low-elasticity cities as a group gained 20 percent in population, that gain was largely the result of Los Angeles being in this category. Most of these cities' annexation activities occurred in the 1950s, and population began to fall thereafter. Sixteen of the twenty-two low-elasticity cities have lost population since peaking by 1960 or later.

Among the twenty-four medium-elasticity cities (which gained 44 percent in population overall), between 1950 and 1990 there were only three net population losers (Evansville and Gary, Indiana, and Birmingham, Alabama). However, seventeen cities whose annexations typically ended around 1970 have already hit their peak populations.

Among the forty-eight high- and hyper-elasticity cities, only Kansas City, Missouri, had a slightly smaller population in 1990

TABLE 2.4
SOME CENTRAL CITIES HAVE GROWN; OTHERS HAVE SHRUNK

Metro Area	Average city population		Percentage change 1950–90
	1950	1990	
Zero-Elasticity	1,086,803	839,411	–23%
Low-Elasticity	344,110	411,462	20
Medium-Elasticity	151,634	217,804	44
High-Elasticity	202,038	449,296	122
Hyper-Elasticity	91,803	320,936	250

than in 1950. (Kansas City annexed massive territory leading out to its international airport, but most new middle-income subdivisions were built on the Kansas side of the Missouri river.) However, a handful may be peaking after having lost population in the past decade.[7]

Of course, all such categorizations of elasticity are based on history. The fact that a central city may have annexed much of its region's new development in the past is no guarantee that it will continue to be elastic in the future. By 1990, however, the truth of Lesson 9 has been demonstrated many times: when a city stops growing, it starts shrinking.

The combined effect of both metropolitan growth and cities' varying elasticity is shown in Table 2.5.

The zero-elasticity group had the largest average number of new-home buyers up for grabs among competing jurisdictions—819,000 persons (about half that group's average metro population in 1950). The low-elasticity group had the second largest number of new-home buyers—667,000 (slightly more than their average metro population in 1950). For the remaining groups the ratio of new-home buyers to average 1950 metro population continues to scale upward proportionally. All metro areas, however, had many new-home buyers for city and suburbs to compete over.

Table 2.6 illustrates the average population density in 1950 of central cities in each group. At 14,003 persons per square mile (238 percent of the national average of 5,873 persons per square mile), the zero-elasticity cities had little vacant land for new, low-density subdivision development; they had no alternative but to expand their boundaries. The low-elasticity cities were also above the national average. But the medium-, high-, and hyper-

TABLE 2.5
ALL GROUPS HAD ABOUT THE SAME NUMBER OF
NEW-HOME BUYERS

Metro Area	New-Home Buyers, 1950–90
Zero-Elasticity	818,853
Low-Elasticity	667,340
Medium-Elasticity	509,559
High-Elasticity	628,985
Hyper-Elasticity	484,703

Table 2.6
High- and Hyper-Elasticity Cities Can Grow through
In-Fill; Lower Elasticity Cities Cannot

City	City density (persons per square miles), 1950	City density as a percentage of the national average, 1950
Zero-Elasticity	14,003	238%
Low-Elasticity	6,676	114
Medium-Elasticity	5,393	92
High-Elasticity	4,833	82
Hyper-Elasticity	5,385	92

elasticity cities had room to grow internally—although they would expand their boundaries dramatically as well.

Table 2.7 demonstrates that double-barrelled advantage. The zero-elasticity cities barely expanded their city limits (3 percent); of the 23 zero-elasticity cities, only two (Philadelphia and Chicago) grew more than two square miles. The low-elasticity cities expanded modestly (20 percent), but the medium-, high-, and hyper-elasticity cities spread far and wide across the landscape.

By 1990 the average zero-elasticity city was the smallest in geographic area (sixty-four square miles), although the group covered a wide range in municipal size—from Paterson, New Jersey (eight square miles), to New York City (309 square miles). By contrast, the average high- or hyper-elasticity city was three or four times as large geographically. Within these latter groups the smallest cities in area were Salinas, Modesto, and Vallejo,

Table 2.7
Elastic Cities Expand Their City Limits;
Inelastic Cities Do Not

City	City area (square miles) 1950	City area (square miles) 1990	Percentage change 1950–90
Zero-Elasticity	68	69	3%
Low-Elasticity	65	78	20
Medium-Elasticity	32	75	138
High-Elasticity	47	179	284
Hyper-Elasticity	17	261	1,402

all in California (eighteen, thirty, and thirty-one square miles, respectively).

The demographic payoff is summed up in Table 2.8, which shows each group's relative "capture/contribute" ratio. Zero-elasticity cities contributed –30 percent of their area's new-home buyers, while low-elasticity cities and medium-elasticity cities captured a modest 10 percent and 13 percent, respectively. High-elasticity cities and hyper-elasticity cities captured major chunks of regional growth (38 and 47 percent, respectively). Zero-elasticity cities are the victims of their suburbs, but high- and hyper-elasticity cities often *are* their own suburbs.

Thus, an examination of the 117 major metro areas testifies again to the first law of urban dynamics: only elastic cities grow.

The social and economic consequences of these striking differences in city-suburb relationships are illustrated in the next several tables. Table 2.9 shows that all groups have roughly the same percentage of Black residents metrowide (from 12 percent to 14 percent). The racial profile of central cities, however, differs substantially.

Hyper-elasticity and zero-elasticity cities are located in metro areas with almost the same proportional population of Blacks. Because of the high concentration of Blacks within the inner city and their substantial exclusion from the suburbs, zero-elasticity cities are 35 percent Black, and their metrowide Black segregation index is a very high 74.

By contrast, hyper-elasticity cities embrace so much of their own suburban development that the proportion of Blacks in the city (17 percent) is not that much higher than the percentage

TABLE 2.8

ELASTIC CITIES "CAPTURE" SUBURBAN GROWTH; INELASTIC CITIES ONLY "CONTRIBUTE" TO SUBURBAN GROWTH

Area/City	City population change 1950–90	Metro new-home buyers 1950–90	City capture/ contribute percentage
Zero-Elasticity	–247,392	818,853	–30%
Low-Elasticity	67,352	667,340	10
Medium-Elasticity	66,170	509,559	13
High-Elasticity	241,625	628,985	38
Hyper-Elasticity	229,133	484,703	47

TABLE 2.9

INELASTIC AREAS ARE MORE SEGREGATED THAN ELASTIC AREAS

Area/City	Percentage Black, 1990		Black segregation index
	Metro	City	
Zero-Elasticity	14%	35%	74
Low-Elasticity	12	24	65
Medium-Elasticity	13	25	64
High-Elasticity	14	22	60
Hyper-Elasticity	13	17	54

metrowide. On a metrowide basis the index of Black segregation at a census tract or neighborhood level is 54 (significantly lower but still unacceptable).

Hispanic concentration and residential segregation follow similar patterns (Table 2.10) although the degree of residential segregation is measurably less for Hispanics than for Blacks.[8] The higher presence of Hispanics metrowide in high- and hyper-elasticity areas (11 percent and 12 percent, respectively) reflects the high degree to which cities in this group are located in California, Florida, and the Southwest—all areas of high Hispanic population.

Economic disparities flow in the same patterns. Table 2.11 analyzes patterns in *nominal* per capita income among the groups. Zero-elasticity areas have the highest average suburban income ($19,194) and the lowest average city income ($12,714); the city-suburb income ratio is 66 percent. By contrast, hyper-elasticity areas have the lowest average suburban income ($14,016) and the highest average city income ($14,221); the city-suburb income ratio is 101 percent.

TABLE 2.10

INELASTIC AREAS THAT SEGREGATE BLACKS
SEGREGATE HISPANICS

Area/City	Percentage Hispanic, 1990		Hispanic Segregation Index
	Metro	City	
Zero-Elasticity	7%	13%	58
Low-Elasticity	7	9	42
Medium-Elasticity	7	10	41
High-Elasticity	11	12	40
Hyper-Elasticity	12	12	38

TABLE 2.11

CITY-SUBURB INCOME GAPS ARE MORE CRITICAL THAN OVERALL METRO
INCOME LEVELS

Area/City	Per capita income, 1989			City-suburb ratio
	Metro	City	Suburb	
Zero-Elasticity	$17,242	$12,714	$19,194	66%
Low-Elasticity	14,684	13,008	15,584	83
Medium-Elasticity	14,553	13,328	15,552	86
High-Elasticity	14,196	13,927	14,452	96
Hyper-Elasticity	14,181	14,221	14,016	101

In Chapter I, I presented several explanations for these disparities in racial and income distribution. I will now review them in the context of this broader analysis.

First, differences in racial and economic segregation are not related to the proportion of Blacks and Hispanics in an area. Areas with high proportions of minorities may be highly segregated or quite well integrated. Similarly, areas with low proportions of minorities may find minorities well blended into the larger community or highly isolated.

Second, although the proportion of minorities metrowide seems to have little to do with the degree of racial segregation, the historic distribution, or racial profile, plays some role. Traditionally, Blacks and Hispanics have lived in rural and small-town areas in the South and West but not in the Northeast and Midwest. As urbanization has reached into the countryside, southern and western cities have not encountered as sharp "racial gradients" as have northeastern and midwestern cities.

Third, the absolute size of the metro area has little effect on the racial and economic isolation of city dwellers. Some of the country's largest cities and metro areas are concentrated within the zero-elasticity category, which suggests that metro and city population size is a factor. However, the relationship of population size to segregation (racial and economic) is weak.

More significant is the "maturity" of the city. Table 2.12 depicts the average date by which cities in each group passed the 100,000 population mark. On average the zero-elasticity cities passed the mark in 1874, the low-elasticity cities passed the mark in 1910, the medium-elasticity cities passed the mark in 1941, and the high-elasticity cities reached the 100,000 inhabitant milestone a year later. The average hyper-elasticity city became a

---

Box 2.3 Montgomery County: Unified Government Unites

Montgomery County, Maryland, is an outstanding example of the progress toward social and economic integration that can be achieved by a unified local government with both the authority and the political will to pursue such goals.

A wealthy suburban county outside Washington, D.C., Montgomery County grew from 164,401 residents in 1950 to 757,027 in 1990, surpassing the nation's capital. The area was a prime candidate for typical suburban balkanization. It did not happen for two reasons.

First, under Maryland state law, the county maintains a single, unified, countywide school system. With 117,068 students in 1994–95, the Montgomery County public school system is among the nation's twenty largest school systems—and clearly one of the best.

Second, in a far-sighted action the Maryland legislature in 1927 (revised in 1939) set up the Maryland-National Capital Park and Planning Commission and gave the Montgomery County government exclusive planning and zoning control throughout the county.[1] This legislative action created "a big enough canvas to work on," Richard Tustian, long-time county planner, once told me. This led to perhaps the nation's most comprehensive growth management system.

Most remarkable is the county's Moderately Priced Dwelling Unit (MPDU) Ordinance. First adopted in 1973, the policy requires builders of fifty or more residential units to set aside 15 percent of the units for low- and moderate-income tenants or buyers. To compensate developers for providing housing below market prices, the county allows a density increase or "MPDU bonus" up to 22 percent above the normal density for the zone. By 1994 more than 9,000 housing units had been created under the policy.

TABLE 2.12

INELASTIC CITIES ARE OLDER THAN ELASTIC CITIES

Area/City	Year when the population exceeded 100,000
Zero-Elasticity	1874
Low-Elasticity	1910
Medium-Elasticity	1941
High-Elasticity	1942
Hyper-Elasticity	1958

Both buyers and renters are subject to maximum income limits set by the County Department of Housing and Community Development. Rent limits are controlled for twenty years. Sale and resale prices for MPDUs are controlled for ten years, and a portion of resale profits is recaptured by the county's revolving Housing Initiative Fund.

MPDUs are sold to individual purchasers. One-third, however, may be purchased by the county public housing authority or by nonprofit organizations for rent to public housing–eligible households.

The MPDU program has helped the county accommodate—and has even encouraged—a remarkable social transformation. In 1970 Montgomery County had the look of a classic suburb—wealthy and White (92 percent). By 1990 Montgomery County had a "rainbow" look—12 percent Black, 7 percent Hispanic, 8 percent Asian. Although Montgomery County is one of the country's richest urban counties, it also has a rich diversity of income groups.

Montgomery County's critics can point to unresolved social problems. But through the decades the Montgomery County government and Montgomery County public schools have demonstrated the ability of broad-based governments to resist the short-term, exclusive "Not-in-My-Backyard" syndrome and to act in the long-term interest of the larger community.

1. The legislature "grandfathered" existing zoning powers for the cities of Rockville and Gaithersburg and five small villages (about 12 percent of the county's population).

"big city" in 1958, well into the dominance of the suburban lifestyle.

A central city's age has many implications. By definition, an old city has an inventory of old, often decaying neighborhoods that typically become home to many poor people. A long-established Black or Hispanic population in an old city may have become highly isolated as victims of the social prejudices of an earlier era. Even an old city's long participation in certain social welfare programs, such as public housing, may reinforce racial and economic isolation. In any event, a city's age strongly influences racial and economic segregation within a metro area.

Finally, a central city's elasticity has the highest relationship of all these factors to the level of racial and economic segregation in a metro area. Why some central cities expanded and others did not must really be the subject of case-by-case studies. My five categories of elasticity bring together many different cities from many different regions, but some general observations can be made.

In general, state laws regarding annexation are less inhibiting in the South and West than they are in the Northeast and Midwest. Old cities (often in the Northeast and Midwest) had more neighbors to contend and compete with than had younger cities (often in the South and West).[9] The lesser "racial gradients" in the South and West raised fewer social and political barriers to a city's outward expansion. And being the hub of a more rapidly growing metro area created a more expansionist outlook among local public officials than was true of political leadership within more slowly expanding areas.

Finally, the relative unity or fragmentation of local government and institutions influences racial and economic segregation. Table 2.13 summarizes the rough picture in terms of local units of general government. The percentage of the area's population that is governed by the central city is listed in the first column. In effect, this statistic tells what proportion of the metro community falls under a single planning and zoning authority.

What does it mean for a zero-elasticity or low-elasticity city to have planning and zoning authority over about one-third of the metro area population? It means little since that city is no

TABLE 2.13
FRAGMENTED LOCAL GOVERNMENT FOSTERS SEGREGATION;
UNIFIED LOCAL GOVERNMENT PROMOTES INTEGRATION

Area/City	Percentage of area population governed by central city	Number of suburban governments	Segregation index	
			Blacks	Hispanics
Zero-Elasticity	35%	131	74	58
Low-Elasticity	31	56	65	42
Medium-Elasticity	26	45	63	41
High-Elasticity	44	55	60	40
Hyper-Elasticity	44	23	54	38

longer planning for new growth that can capture a share of the middle-class, suburban-style population.

By contrast, it is significant when a high- or hyper-elasticity city represents 40 percent or more of the area because that city is planning for and capturing more than half of the area's suburban-style growth. How an elastic city government shapes the mix and distribution of new housing, new shopping areas, and new business parks makes a big difference in the future racial and economic profile of the area.

At first glance, the number of suburban governments in zero-elasticity metro areas is three-to-six times higher than in more elastic metro areas. But after correcting for the larger population size of zero-elasticity areas, the fragmentation of suburban government drops to about a two-to-one ratio.

Nevertheless, the fragmentation of planning and zoning authority among multiple suburban governments in zero-elasticity areas is serious because these suburban governments are planning for all of the area's new growth. Balkanization of the suburbs inevitably promotes exclusive planning and zoning. By contrast, the lesser balkanization of the suburbs around more elastic cities is less significant because these independent, suburban governments are typically planning for less than half of the area's expansion.

The data in Table 2.13 must be treated with caution because they are a rough approximation of reality. What does an average of 131 suburban governments in zero-elasticity metro areas really mean? What are the planning and zoning powers of municipalities? Of townships? Of county governments? Must local governments zone in accordance with some areawide plan? The answers will vary from state to state.

In Table 2.13 I assume all units of local government have planning and zoning powers. That is certainly wrong. As a description of almost any specific metro area, that assumption is inaccurate.[10] As a characterization of an important factor shaping urban America, I believe that the observation is valid.

Table 2.14 relates the relative unity or fragmentation of public education to racial segregation in public school systems metrowide. In contrast to residential segregation, segregation of Black students in more elastic areas is lower than it is in zero-elasticity areas. This is because public education in many southern states is characterized by large countywide school systems that operate under long-standing racial integration plans. This

TABLE 2.14
DISPERSED AND FRAGMENTED PUBLIC EDUCATION IS MORE
SEGREGATED THAN CENTRALIZED AND UNIFIED PUBLIC EDUCATION

Metro Area	Percentage of metro area students enrolled in city schools	Average number of suburban school districts*	School segregation index	
			Blacks	Hispanics
Zero-Elasticity	24%	73	74	61
Low-Elasticity	35	32	63	46
Medium-Elasticity	41	20	58	44
High-Elasticity	44	25	50	41
Hyper-Elasticity	50	20	45	38

*That maintain high schools.

has meant that southern schools are more integrated than southern neighborhoods. (Absent similar integration plans for Hispanic students, there is no such divergence between school segregation levels and neighborhood segregation levels for Hispanics.)

Do these differences in the degree of fragmentation of local government and local education help explain the differences in racial and economic segregation among different metro areas? I believe they do based both on my analysis and on personal experience as an elected public official.

It matters whether a mayor or school board member shaping local policy sees poor Blacks, Hispanics, and Asians as "our people here" or "those people there." Too often suburban officials (and they are usually White) see "those people there," when they look at the declining, decaying, impoverished, minority-dominated inner city. Too often city officials (and they are increasingly Black and Hispanic) see "those people there" when they look at the still overwhelmingly White "outer city." In a more unified area a mayor or school board member will see both groups as common constituents, (hopefully) as both deserving to be served in a fair and equitable way.

Lacking the precision with which the data support the first law of urban dynamics, I would argue that the evidence from the 117 metro areas supports the second law of urban dynamics: fragmentation divides; unification unites.

What is the interaction between economic trends and these patterns of metro development? Table 2.15 outlines the growth

---

Box 2.4 Complete Package Sells Albuquerque's Economy

As mayor of Albuquerque, I had many meetings with national corporations that were considering Albuquerque as a location for business expansion. What business was looking for was not cheap, nonunion labor. What business valued—and what we successfully sold them—was a total community package:

- an available labor force, reasonably prepared, very trainable, highly motivated, and with minimal racial and class antagonisms;
- a decent public school system (in Albuquerque's case, a metrowide system, whose operations are financed by state government, and whose capital construction is financed by a metrowide property tax levy);
- a respectable state university and a superb, business-oriented, technical-vocational institute (also funded by the state and by a metrowide tax levy);
- available, reasonably priced land, industrial bond financing (which almost all states now authorize), good transportation networks, and excellent energy supplies;
- a highly competent city government, adequately financed at moderate tax rates, with a tax base covering 80 percent of all residential property, and 90 percent of all commercial and industrial property in the metro area; and
- a livable, relaxed quality of life (although for some newcomers, New Mexico's high desert scenery and climate take getting used to).

These characteristics are by no means unique to Albuquerque. They typify the elastic communities I have been discussing.

And for Albuquerque they paid off in thousands of new jobs in high-tech manufacturing and regional and national business service centers.

---

of jobs in terms of city-suburb income ratios and rates of growth. As expected, job growth parallels the trends in population growth. The higher the rate of regional population growth, the higher the rate of job creation. As with overall population, the absolute increase in jobs created has been substantial in all groups.

The relationship between a central city's economic health and its suburbs' economic health has provoked lively debate in recent years. Many suburbanites believe they are economically in-

Table 2.15
Elastic Areas Have Faster Rates of Job Creation
than Inelastic Areas

Metro Area	City/suburb per capita income rate, 1989	Metro job growth, 1973–88
Zero-Elasticity	66%	23%
Low-Elasticity	83	39
Medium-Elasticity	86	57
High-Elasticity	96	60
Hyper-Elasticity	101	71

dependent of the city. Certainly there are many examples of highly prosperous individual suburban communities outside the most depressed central cities, like Bloomfield Hills outside Detroit. And with the increasing migration of jobs to suburban office complexes and industrial parks, many argue that "edge cities" are the wave of the future and that the old central cities may be abandoned.

The bulk of evidence, however, supports the view that cities and suburbs are "all in it together." All are part of a regional economy whose overall fortunes are shaped primarily by constant changes in technology, consumer tastes, competition (increasingly global), transportation and communications linkages, investment capital flows, labor force quality, and other economic forces.

One dramatic economic trend in recent decades has been the "deindustrialization" of the American economy. In 1950, for example, the largest segment of the American workforce—33 percent—was engaged in manufacturing; by 1990 the percentage of manufacturing workers had dropped to 18 percent (and many of these workers were not production employees but designers, engineers, marketing executives, and accountants working for manufacturing companies).

Trends in manufacturing jobs (Table 2.16) reveal that deindustrialization has hit inelastic areas hard. Though manufacturing's share of employment has dropped steadily since 1950, the number of industrial jobs grew in almost all metro areas until the early 1970s. Between 1973 and 1988 the zero-elasticity group lost 1.3 million manufacturing jobs (a –22 percent drop). The low-elasticity group also dropped slightly (–2 percent), but manufacturing jobs increased in medium-, high-, and hyper-elastic-

TABLE 2.16
ELASTIC AREAS ADJUST BETTER TO ECONOMIC CHANGE THAN DO INELASTIC
AREAS

| Metro Area | Percentage of metro jobs in manufacturing | | Change in manufacturing jobs 1973–88 |
	1973	1988	
Zero-Elasticity	22%	14%	–22%
Low-Elasticity	22	16	–2
Medium-Elasticity	19	13	6
High-Elasticity	17	12	15
Hyper-Elasticity	16	13	41

ity metro areas. For all 117 metro areas, manufacturing employment slid downward from 12.2 million to 11.5 million jobs (a loss of about –5.5 percent).

Clearly, there is a regional pattern here. Is the deindustrialization of one part of the country and the modest industrialization of another part a simple Frostbelt-Sunbelt phenomenon? In part, yes. Most of the old, smokestack industries that have been driven out of business by international competition have been located in the Northeast or industrial Midwest. Jobs in certain industries (for example, steel and aluminum), once lost, are not re-created elsewhere in the country.

Urban areas, however, are not simply passive beneficiaries or victims of economic changes. Local areas can shape their futures. Detroit, for example, may have lost massive numbers of auto industry jobs, but other areas of the country have added automotive jobs (for example, Arlington, Texas, in the Dallas-Ft. Worth area; Smyrna, Tennessee, in the Nashville-Murfreesboro area; or Greenville-Spartanburg, South Carolina). An aging plant may be closed as obsolete, but its home region need not lose its replacement.[12] Moreover, an area can certainly nurture or compete for new businesses, based on new types of products and new types of services, which are the basis of most new "export product" jobs.

Each region has attractions in terms of the lifestyle it can offer. The Sunbelt does not have an inherent advantage over the Frostbelt. Many old cities, for example, have cultural facilities and institutions that are superior to those in newer cities. Climate and geography are matters of taste and adjustment. Inelastic areas are not without intrinsic competitive advantages.

What many inelastic areas have lost is the ability to compete. Business seeks out labor markets and economic regions, rarely specific governmental jurisdictions. But economic development is a private-public partnership, and the capabilities of the public partner are vital. Typically, a strong, healthy, elastic central city is a metropolitan area's dominant and most capable public partner. This type of city has broad planning and zoning powers (often with extraterritorial planning jurisdiction) and often directly owns major infrastructure systems (e.g., water supply and sewage treatment). With its broad tax base, an elastic city can finance the public infrastructure needed to support major private investment. And it has the power to make major decisions. As Harvey Gannt, former mayor of high-elastic Charlotte, has observed, metro areas "with fewer governmental entities have a definite advantage in quicker decision making, building regional consensus, and moving forward on large initiatives."[11]

By contrast, who speaks and acts for greater Detroit or greater Cleveland, suffering from high political fragmentation, strong racial divisions, sharp income differentials, interjurisdictional competition—in short, from the loss of a shared sense of community and common destiny metrowide?

The economic data on the five categories of elasticity do show regional biases. Most inelastic areas are in the Northeast and Midwest; most elastic areas are in the South and West. When examining nominal rates of poverty metrowide (Table 2.17), we see that slightly higher percentages of the population of high-elasticity and hyper-elasticity areas fall under the poverty level than

TABLE 2.17

POVERTY IS MORE CONCENTRATED IN INELASTIC CITIES THAN IN ELASTIC CITIES

Metro Area	Percentage of metro population below the poverty line, 1990	Percentage of city population below the poverty line, 1990	City's fair share index of metro area poor population, 1990
Zero-Elasticity	10%	22%	228%
Low-Elasticity	12	19	167
Medium-Elasticity	12	18	153
High-Elasticity	13	17	127
Hyper-Elasticity	14	15	114

occurs in zero-, low-, and medium-elasticity areas. One might conclude from this that the former group of communities is less effective at reducing poverty than the latter, but poverty levels have historically been higher in the South and West. In recent decades the rate of reduction of poverty has been greater in these regions as well (although somewhat slowed by the accelerating pace of immigration).

What is more critical for the health of central cities is that poverty is much more concentrated in inelastic cities than in elastic cities. Inelastic cities are cast in the role of home for most of their metro areas' poor minorities, as clearly indicated by disparities in the central cities' fair share of poverty index. Zero-elasticity cities have exactly twice the fair share of poverty (228 percent) that hyper-elasticity cities have (114 percent). Moreover, elastic cities' lesser concentration of poverty by jurisdiction is not just an artifact of these cities being larger proportions of their metro areas. Elastic cities also have somewhat less concentration of poverty on a neighborhood by neighborhood basis. Controlling planning, zoning, and housing policy for a larger portion of the region, elastic cities have the capacity to help spread low- and moderate-income housing across a wide range of neighborhoods.

An even more complex picture is presented in Table 2.18, which shows the rate of growth in real median family income metrowide over a forty-year period (1949–89). By my hypothesis, progress in real incomes should be least in zero-elasticity areas and scale steadily upward to the highest rates in hyper-elasticity areas. Instead, with 123 percent growth in real family incomes, the zero-elasticity group outperformed the low-

TABLE 2.18

REAL METRO INCOME GROWTH HAS BEEN GREATER
IN ELASTIC AREAS THAN IN INELASTIC AREAS

Metro Area	Percentage growth in real family income metrowide, 1949–89	Percentage growth in real family income in central city, 1949–89
Zero-Elasticity	123%	62%
Low-Elasticity	108	62
Medium-Elasticity	127	84
High-Elasticity	134	96
Hyper-Elasticity	139	111

Box 2.5 Ties That Bind City and Suburbs

Two recent studies have examined the degree of interdependence of city and suburban economies.

Professor H. V. Savitch of the University of Louisville argues that "self-sufficiency neither was nor will be a modus operandi for cities and suburbs. As time goes by, interdependence, resource synergy and the ability to interact beyond exclusive spheres become important for metropolitan success. To do otherwise is to put suburbs at the edge of a sinkhole, whose slopes may be slippery."[1]

Savitch analyzed fifty-nine large metro areas. Those with central cities in the top income quartile generated over $2,000 more income per year per suburban resident than cities in the lowest quartile. Despite the impression of increasingly solitary suburbs, between 1979 and 1987 the interdependence became stronger. "A decade ago 47 percent of suburban income could be attributed to the density and income of the central city," Professor Savitch writes. "Today, that number has risen to 61 percent. Translated into earning capacity, for every $1,000 difference in city per capita income, suburbs stand to gain or lose $690."

Savitch also studied seven large central cities. The earnings generated by these cities rose in 1969–89, and the suburban share increased substantially in Baltimore, Denver, New Orleans, and Washington, D.C. Philadelphia's suburbanites increased their share of central city earnings modestly, while in St. Louis and San Francisco suburbanites maintained their share of central city

---

elasticity group (108 percent), though lagged behind the more elastic metro areas (127 to 139 percent).

Closer examination shows that average real income growth for the zero-elasticity group was buoyed by the powerful economic performances of America's flagship, postindustrial regions, in the corridor from Boston to Washington, D.C. Almost sealed off from surrounding neighborhoods, the traditional downtowns continued as national and international centers of financial, information, government, and business services. Around the outlying beltways other information-age businesses blossomed. As metropolitan regions they maintained their national economic leadership.

For many, however, life within their cities deteriorated. Lacking necessary skills and ready transportation, many residents of inelastic cities did not benefit from downtown office jobs (skill barriers) or beltway-centered, high-tech manufacturing jobs earnings. For all seven areas suburbanites accounted for between 34 percent (Philadelphia) and 63 percent (Washington, D.C.) of all earnings generated in central cities.

Savitch concluded that "whether cities are prosperous, what they do and how they do it matters. These conditions can mean the difference between metropolitan prosperity or decline. . . . Suburbs which surround healthy cities stand a better chance of vitality than those that surround sick cities. . . . Self-sufficiency at the periphery is not a sufficient defense. The challenge of repair is as much for those outside the center as for those in it."

In a study of 28 metro areas in the Northeast and Middle West, Richard Voith, a senior economist for the Federal Reserve Bank of Philadelphia, also found high correlations in growth of real incomes and employment between central city and suburban economies. He concluded that "decline in central cities is likely to be associated with slow-growing suburbs. Even if the most acute problems associated with urban decline do not arise in the suburbs, central city decline is likely to be a long-run, slow drain on the economic and social vitality of the region."[2]

1. H. V. Savitch, "Ties That Bind: Central Cities, Suburbs and the New Metropolitan Region." Economic Development Quarterly 7 (November 1993): 341–57.
2. Richard Voith, "City and Suburban Growth: Substitutes or Complements?" in the Business Review of the Federal Reserve Bank of Philadelphia, September–October 1992, p. 31.

(skill and transportation barriers). Gaps between income classes tended to grow wider within such regions.

From city hall's perspective, municipal bond ratings remain a key indicator of a city's long-term economic health (Table 2.19).

TABLE 2.19
ELASTIC CITIES HAVE BETTER BOND RATINGS THAN DO
INELASTIC CITIES

City	City bond rating*
Zero-Elasticity	5.43
Low-Elasticity	6.40
Medium-Elasticity	7.21
High-Elasticity	8.03
Hyper-Elasticity	6.76

*Numerical values assigned to Moody's bond ratings are AAA=10.0; AA=8.0; A=6.0; BAA=4.0; BA=2.0; and B=1.0.

Although zero-elasticity cities are in the wealthiest metro areas (nominally), they have bond ratings that are lower than their municipal counterparts in other categories. High-elasticity cities have the highest bond ratings; in general their economies are more fully developed and mature than are the economies of hyper-elasticity areas that are growing even more spectacularly.

The Point of No Return

Table 2.20 focuses on twenty-four cities that by 1990 had passed the "point of no return" that I defined in Chapter I. All twenty-four cities experienced major population loss (–20 percent or more), had a disproportionate minority population (typically, 30 percent or more), and, most important, their residents had average income levels that were less than 70 percent of suburban income levels. In addition, another ten cities met the criteria regarding disproportionate minority population and city-suburban income gap, but they had not suffered such major population loss. In most cases, increased Hispanic immigration had blunted the impact of the middle-class White and Black exodus.

Past the point of no return, city-suburb economic disparities become so severe that, in a broad sense, the city is no longer a place in which to invest or to create jobs (with the exception of fortress-like downtown business districts). During the 1980s all twenty-four cities lost economic ground to their suburbs. In twelve of the twenty-four—Holyoke, Flint, Birmingham, Saginaw, Youngstown, Atlantic City, East Chicago, Gary, Detroit, Trenton, Benton Harbor, and North Chicago—the income gap expanded at disastrous, double-digit rates. Overall, the income levels of the twenty-four cities dropped from 68 percent to 58 percent of suburban levels.

The minority percentage of all 24 cities also climbed rapidly (from 55 percent to 59 percent)—a disproportionate 3-to-1 ratio within their metro areas. The increase was more a result of the continuing exodus of Whites (along with middle-class Blacks and Hispanics) rather than of increasing numbers of minority poor.

Finally, in the 1980s twenty of the twenty-four cities continued to lose population with only Holyoke, New Haven, Hartford, and Camden halting their population decline (at least during the last decade—all because of Hispanic, mostly Puerto Rican, immigration).

Cities past the point of no return are not hopeless. However, they cannot escape the grip of ghetto poverty solely by their own efforts. Despite the redevelopment projects, enterprise zones, and neighborhood empowerment programs, *no city past the point of no return has ever closed the economic gap with its suburbs by as much as a single percentage point!* Isolated within their metro areas, decade by decade cities past the point of no return demonstrate the fourth law of urban dynamics: ghettos only become bigger ghettos.

Cities without Suburbs

The cities in Table 2.20 are doing very poorly even though many are located in some of the country's nominally wealthiest areas. This section examines the other extreme—cities that are doing well even though they are located in more modest-income metro areas. These are all cities that dominate their areas. They are, in effect, cities without suburbs (see Table 2.21).

I have applied two standards to identify a city without suburbs. First, the city must house 50 percent or more of the metro population. On this basis, for example, prominent cities like San Diego, Charlotte, and Houston miss the cut. Second, the average per capita income of city residents must be 90 percent or more of the average per capita income of suburban residents. Below this standard continual suburbanization of the middle class is occurring. San Antonio, San Jose, and Tucson represent 70 percent or more of their metro populations; however, average incomes within the three cities have fallen to about 72 percent of suburban levels. This widening income gap excludes them from the table and suggests significant future problems for all three cities.

Twenty-three cities meet my cities-without-suburbs criteria. Five are consolidated governments: Nashville-Davidson; Indianapolis-Marion; Lexington-Fayette, Kentucky; Jacksonville-Duval, Florida; and Columbus-Muskogee, Georgia. The others have maintained their dominance of the local area through aggressive annexation policies.

None of these communities is paradise. None is exempt from the social problems of modern-day America. To the eyes of some residents of the nation's more glamorous and cosmopolitan centers, these twenty-three may appear to be modest communities that (in Winston Churchill's words) "have much to be modest

TABLE 2.20

For Inelastic Cities Past the Point of No Return, the Population Continues to Decline, the Minority Ratio Continues to Increase, and the City-Suburb Income Gap Continues to Widen

City	Change in city population*		Percentage of minorities in city		City-suburb income ratio	
	By 1980	By 1990	1980	1990	1979	1989
Holyoke, Mass.	-26%	-26%	16%	35%	86%	69%
BUFFALO, N.Y.	-37	-43	35	37	77	69
FLINT, Mich.	-19	-29	49	52	84	69
BIRMINGHAM, Ala.	-15	-22	59	64	79	69
ST. LOUIS, Mo.	-47	-54	50	50	71	67
SAGINAW, Mich.	-21	-29	44	50	81	66
CHICAGO, Ill.	-17	-23	57	60	69	66
YOUNGSTOWN, Ohio	-32	-44	34	35	83	64
DAYTON, Ohio	-26	-31	35	36	72	64
PHILADELPHIA, Pa.	-19	-23	42	45	72	64
BALTIMORE, Md.	-17	-23	57	60	68	64
NEW HAVEN, Conn.	-23	-21	44	47	70	62

City						
ATLANTIC CITY, N.J.	−39	−43	61	69	77	61
East Chicago, Ind.	−31	−41	N/A	81	74	60
Gary, Ind.	−15	−25	81	85	71	59
CLEVELAND, Ohio	−37	−45	48	50	63	54
HARTFORD, Conn.	−23	−21	61	66	62	53
DETROIT, Mich.	−35	−44	69	77	67	53
Trenton, N.J.	−28	−31	54	59	65	50
Benton Harbor, Mich.	−23	−33	88	93	54	43
Newark, N.J.	−26	−38	77	82	48	42
North Chicago, Ill.	−18	−26	32	47	50	39
Camden, N.J.	−32	−30	72	86	47	39
East St. Louis, Ill.	−33	−50	97	98	44	39

(Kansas City, Kansas; Petersburg, Va.; Milwaukee, Wisc.; Bessemer, Ala.; Pontiac, Mich.; Chicago Heights, Ill.; Bridgeport, Conn.; and Elizabeth, Paterson, and Perth Amboy, N.J., have not yet lost more than 20% of population but have passed critical thresholds of disproportionate minority population and have a large income gap.)

Note: Cities in uppercase letters are considered to be the primary or historic central city for their metro area. Cities in lowercase letters are considered to be secondary central cities.

*Population changes are measured from the city's peak population.

Box 2.6 Research Documents Black Ghetto Expansion

In a study of 318 metro areas between 1980 and 1990, Paul Jargowsky, a University of Texas at Dallas social scientist, has found that Black ghetto poverty has increased significantly.[1]

Defining a Black ghetto as an urban census tract in which 40 percent or more of the Black population is poor (in 1989, an income of less than $10,360 for a family of three), Jargowsky found that the number of Blacks living in ghetto areas increased 36 percent from 4.3 million to 5.9 million.

The percentage of the total Black population living in ghetto areas increased from 20 percent to almost 24 percent—which, however, means that over three-quarters of the Black population does not live in urban ghettos.

On the other hand, poor Blacks are increasingly isolated from the Black middle class in urban ghettos. The proportion of poor urban Blacks in ghetto areas increased from 37 percent to 45 percent while, on the average, poor households edged past the fifty percent level in such areas for the first time.

Most ominous for many city officials, the physical size of urban ghettos expanded dramatically during the 1980s even as, with the flight of the Black middle class to suburbs, the population density of ghettos declined. The number of census tracts classified as ghettos grew from 3,256 to 5,003—a 54 percent increase!—while population density declined –11 percent in ghetto areas.

"From the point of view of local political officials, the increase in the size of the ghetto is a disaster," Jargowsky comments. "Many of those leaving the ghetto settle in nonghetto areas outside the political jurisdiction of the central city. Thus, the geographic size of the ghetto is expanding, cutting a wider swath through the hearts of our metropolitan areas."

---

about." And yet, both as cities and as whole metro areas they are doing pretty well. With the exception of Anchorage, all have average or below average costs of living, as a group their cost-of-living index is 95 (5 percent below the national urban average). This means that their residents' nominal incomes (as reported by the census) stretch farther than the higher incomes reported in high-cost regions, such as the Boston-to-Washington corridor or the San Francisco-to-San Diego corridor.

In essence, these twenty-three cities dominated their metropolitan areas in 1990, averaging 65 percent of their regional populations. Residents of cities without suburbs might be expected

Jargowsky finds that ghetto poverty is a function of both racial segregation and metropolitan economic growth. During the 1980s, the proportion of Blacks living in ghettos increased most dramatically in the declining industrial states and oil patch communities caught in the oil and real estate slump. By contrast, booming, postindustrial economies around Boston, Hartford, New York, Philadelphia, Baltimore, and Washington allowed many middle-class Blacks to leave ghettos for new suburban homes.

"Ghetto poverty," Jargowsky concludes, "is not primarily the product of a 'ghetto culture' that discourages upward mobility, but the product of metropolitan labor markets and residential settlement patterns. Ghetto self-help programs, enterprise zones, etc., cannot alter the fundamental dynamics of metropolitan economies or the evolving geography of residential location decisions.

"Vigorous enforcement of antidiscrimination in housing, scatter-site public housing, and zoning requirements that encourage mixed-income developments can all play a role in reducing the segregation of Blacks and the Black poor," Jargowsky recommends. "This has both an immediate effect-reducing ghetto poverty-and an indirect, long-term effect-the increased earnings potential of children who attend better schools, grow up in safer, more stimulating environments, and see better role models of success in the mainstream economy."

1. Paul A. Jargowsky, "Ghetto Poverty among Blacks in the 1980s" (January 15, 1993; unpublished paper). *U.S. News and World Report* reported Jargowsky's findings in an article entitled "The Shifting State of Black Ghettos" (January 18, 1993).

to be better off than residents of less elastic cities that are a smaller share of their regions' populations (32 percent) and where many of the wealthy have fled to their suburbs. In 1989 the residents of cities without suburbs had incomes 6 percent above suburban levels, while in the other ninety-four cities average incomes were 13 percent below that of their suburbs. Adjusted for differences in cost of living, real median family income translated into $35,841 for residents of cities without suburbs compared with $29,234 for residents of the other ninety-four central cities—a 23 percent higher standard of living for residents of cities without suburbs. The economic strength of

TABLE 2.21
TWENTY-THREE CITIES WITHOUT SUBURBS

Metro Area	Percentage of metro area residents living in city, 1990	City-suburb income ratio, 1989	Real median family income of metro residents, 1989	Change in per capita income, 1969–89	Residential segregation index for Blacks	1993 city bond rating*
Jackson, Miss.	50%	99%	$35,881	44%	67	6.00
Nashville-Davidson, Tenn.	50	98	37,681	49	61	10.00
Madison, Wis.	52	95	39,551	34	48	10.00
Tulsa, Okla.	52	129	37,881	32	62	8.00
Reno, Nev.	53	97	34,129	26	37	5.50
Fresno, Calif.	53	95	27,245	27	52	5.50
Tallahassee, Fla.	53	102	37,885	37	52	6.00
Omaha, Nebr.-Iowa	54	95	40,206	31	70	10.00
Shreveport, La.	59	103	32,293	37	60	6.00
Indianapolis-Marion, Ind.	59	90	39,989	32	74	10.00
Austin, Tex.	60	96	37,066	51	56	6.00

TABLE 2.21 CONTINUED

Metro Area	Percentage of metro area residents living in city, 1990	City-suburb income ratio, 1989	Real median family income of metro residents, 1989	Change in per capita income, 1969–89	Residential segregation index for Blacks	1993 city bond rating*
Wichita, Kans.	63	104	41,780	52	64	8.00
Montgomery, Ala.	64	112	36,009	44	60	6.00
Lexington-Fayette, Ky.	65	124	36,335	41	54	6.00
Huntsville, Ala.	67	117	40,900	46	57	8.00
Jacksonville-Duval, Fla.	70	90	36,080	50	58	6.00
Colorado Springs, Colo.	71	116	36,098	39	44	8.50
Corpus Christi, Tex.	74	129	30,977	34	56	5.50
Columbus-Muskogee, Ga.-Ala.	74	127	33,455	34	58	6.00
Albuquerque, N. Mex.	80	118	31,701	41	39	8.00
Lubbock, Tex.	84	118	35,326	31	60	8.00
Lincoln, Nebr.	90	94	40,074	30	43	8.00
Anchorage, Alaska	100	100	39,760	39	35	6.00
94 Other Metro Area-Means	31%	87%	$36,448	34%	65	6.54*
23 Cities without Suburbs-Means	65	106	$35,369	38	55	7.26

*Numerical values assigned to Moody's bond ratings are AAA=10.0; AA=8.0; A=6.0; BAA=4.0; BA=2.0; and B=1.0.

these cities was reflected in somewhat better municipal bond ratings (7.26, or almost AA); none of the twenty-three cities had less than an A1 rating.

But as shown in Table 2.21, the average resident of the twenty-three metro areas also had a higher real median family income ($36,448) than the average resident of the other ninety-four areas ($35,369), including all the latter group's wealthier, more exclusive suburban enclaves. And over a recent twenty-year period (1969–89), the twenty-three metro areas were widening their advantage with a real growth rate (38 percent) higher than the real growth rate of the other ninety-four areas (34 percent).

The key, I believe, is that these twenty-three communities are becoming societies of greater social equity and economic mobility. They have a lower level of racial segregation—55 compared with 65—still far, however, from being truly integrated societies. Since these cities have greater unity among their public institutions, their residents have better access to the entire region's resources than the residents of regions of more fragmented governance.

In short, however modest cities without suburbs may appear on the world stage, they are making more of their region's available resources. What would happen if more fragmented regions, particularly their inelastic inner cities, could harness the resources and opportunities of their entire regions? Chapter III discusses some of the possibilities.

Notes

1. These smaller metro areas are "free-standing" areas, not outlying regions of larger metropolitan areas, except Racine, Wisconsin (part of the greater Milwaukee area), and Vineland-Millville-Bridgeton, New Jersey (part of the greater Philadelphia area). Except for many metro areas located in Florida, Texas, and California, these smaller metro areas are relatively slow-growing urban nodes, small manufacturing communities, or commercial centers for agricultural and natural resource regions. In 1950 only 9 out of the 131 areas (Amarillo and Waco, Texas; Asheville, North Carolina; Cedar Rapids, Iowa; Decatur and Springfield, Illinois; Pueblo, Colorado; St. Joseph, Missouri; and Topeka, Kansas) were considered important enough by the Census Bureau to rank as Metropolitan Areas. Most of the nine have quietly—and perhaps not unhappily—watched the world pass them by.

2. Charleston, West Virginia, is an exception. Its vigorous economic prosperity is largely the result of Charleston's having developed a replacement resource for coal—U.S. Senator Robert Byrd's influence in directing federal spending to projects in his state.

3. Of course, "White-only metro areas" are not discrimination-free communities. Interestingly, however, none of these metro areas has developed a significant income gap between the central city and the suburbs. The city-suburb income ratios range between 94 percent (Manchester-Nashua, New Hampshire) and 119 percent (Boise, Idaho). Through annexation their central cities (omitting New England) have expanded vigorously in area (153 percent) and moderately in population (63 percent). The very absence of city-suburb income gaps and elasticity-limiting conditions suggests the role that racial issues play as drivers of urban growth patterns and city-suburb disparities in many other metro areas.

4. In the first edition of *Cities without Suburbs* I gave equal weight to initial density and boundary expansion. Through further statistical analysis I found that assigning three times greater importance to boundary expansion better "fit" a central city's capture/contribute ratio. The effect is to emphasize the importance of annexation and city/county consolidation in a city's relative elasticity ranking.

5. Although these categories represent groupings by decile, they contain uneven numbers of metro areas (for example, twenty-two low-elasticity areas and twenty-five hyper-elasticity areas.) The reason is that the elasticity scores were calculated for all 522 central cities, split into three different sizes. The apparent unevenness of the categories results from my decision to deal with only one central city in a metro area. For example, Scottsdale, Tempe, and Mesa, Arizona, are all hyper-elastic central cities in the Phoenix metro area, but they are not added to the hyper-elastic category because Phoenix is the only central city treated in my analysis for that metro area.

6. The Pittsburgh, New York, Jersey City, and St. Joseph, Missouri, areas were the only metro areas, except for the "Declining mining regions," actually to lose population (–8, –1, –15 and –14 percent, respectively). The New York-northern New Jersey-Connecticut CMSA gained 4 million people, or 29 percent.

7. In addition to Kansas City, high- and hyper-elastic cities that have recently lost population are Macon, Georgia; Shreveport, Louisiana; Chattanooga, Tennessee; Jackson, Mississippi; Mobile, Alabama; Little Rock, Arkansas; and Indianapolis-Marion County, though only Kansas City, Macon, and Chattanooga's populations have declined by more than 5 percent.

8. Of necessity, as in Chapter I, I have used school segregation indices for Hispanics where residential segregation indices have not been calculated by the census bureau.

9. Having already been surrounded by smaller municipalities is the largest single factor preventing further expansion by the oldest, zero-elastic "giants" of the Northeast and Midwest. That does not explain the relative inelasticity of many older cities other than New York, Chicago, Detroit, Philadelphia, and Boston. Moreover, racial and political motives to "contain" the old cities often played a role in the founding of old suburbs as well.

10. Consider the example of Albuquerque. My data show that the Albuquerque area has a central city covering 80 percent of the population, with three suburban governments covering the remaining 20 percent. In reality, two of the three suburban governments are tiny municipalities that account for less than 3 percent of the metro area's population. There are only two planning and zoning authorities of consequence: the city of Albuquerque and Bernalillo County. For years Bernalillo County contracted with the city for professional planning services. Both adopted a common Comprehensive Growth Plan. In the case of a se-

rious dispute, the city can invoke extraterritorial planning and zoning powers within five miles of its city limits.

In short, each metro area has its own story to tell, which is why my statistical characterization is true in the large, but never wholly accurate in the small.

11. Harvey B. Gannt, "A Tale of Two Cities: Charlotte's Regional Approach Means Fast Decisions, Fast Results," in "Turning Point," a special section of the *Boston Globe,* October 30, 1994, p. 28.

12. The city of Detroit has recently succeeded in getting automakers to build two new plants for six thousand workers (at the cost of tremendous public subsidies) but is losing headquarters jobs to its suburbs.

Chapter III

Strategies for Stretching Cities

Reversing the fragmentation of urban areas is an essential step in ending severe racial and economic segregation. The "city" must be redefined to reunify city and suburb. Ideally, such reunification is achieved through metropolitan government.

Four Strategies

The most important benefits of unification can be achieved if local governments adopt (or are required to follow) four strategies: end fiscal imbalance through revenue sharing between rich and poor jurisdictions; diminish racial and economic segregation through affordable housing requirements and housing assistance programs metrowide; promote metrowide economic development; and, finally, implement regional growth management policies.

Revenue sharing alone is inadequate; no amount of money can salvage isolated inner cities. Areawide housing programs are slow to take hold and most effective within a vigorously growing economy. A beltway-centered and downtown-centered economic boom does not trickle down to inner city ghettos and barrios. Unfettered urban sprawl promotes economic segregation and constantly threatens inelastic cities and older suburbs with slow abandonment. All four strategies are inseparable and indispensable parts of a successful approach.

Having a metropolitan government is much better than trying to get multiple local governments to act like a metropolitan government. The former is a more lasting and stable framework for sustained, long-term action.

End Fiscal Imbalance

By taxing a larger share of the wealth of metro areas, a metro government matches resources to problems. Metropolitanization eliminates local fiscal imbalances under which inner cities, grappling with the lion's share of social problems, face dwindling tax resources.

From the perspective of fiscal equalization, the case for metro government is quite clear. The benefits would flow automatically from metropolitanization.

Diminish Racial and Economic Segregation

Through planning and zoning powers and government housing assistance plans, a local government can help shape where different economic classes live. A broad-based government is not generally as afflicted with the "Not-in-My-Backyard" syndrome as is a narrow-based government. A broad-based government can carry out zoning policies and capital outlay plans that encourage the private market to bring more mixed-income neighborhoods into being. Within its wide jurisdiction a broad-based government is able to scatter public housing projects and implement rent subsidy programs across a variety of neighborhoods. It is, in effect, able to follow strategies of dispersion of low-income groups, if it chooses, and, through dispersion, to reduce the very severity and incidence of social stress.

That a metro government would pursue automatically such policies is not guaranteed. What is clear, however, is that a highly fragmented metro area has little ability to agree on socially controversial policies, absent powerful compulsion by state or federal law.

Promote Areawide Economic Progress

Metro areas with a dominant government have a more cohesive community spirit. More effective public-private coalitions form to promote common interests. Internecine warfare among local jurisdictions is minimized, in particular, when revenue-sharing arrangements allow all communities to share benefits from new growth. Such genuine communities are able to compete on the terms the marketplace most values—namely, as integrated, total labor market areas.

CONTROL URBAN SPRAWL

In larger metro areas, multijurisdictional growth-control powers must flow to local governments from state law. However, within smaller, single-county metro areas, a metropolitan government usually will be endowed with sufficient powers under state law to adopt reasonable growth management policies. Beyond meeting larger environmental goals, growth management policies can ensure more balanced development, conserving the value of older residential and commercial areas and promoting mixed-income housing in newer subdivisions.

Is advocating metro government a feasible strategy? Successfully challenging racial and class attitudes undergirding the fragmentation of many urban areas is the toughest political task in America. To that daunting challenge must be added overcoming the stolid inertia of the status quo. In fact, widespread skepticism among the "experts" may be the greatest initial barrier to implementing my proposals. The slow progress of voluntary regional cooperation and the few successful efforts at forming metro governments have made many planners skeptical about reform. Who can seriously advocate metro government for New York, Chicago, Philadelphia, or Detroit, for example?

My proposals should not be judged by how immediately feasible they might be for the hardest cases. The United States of America is a big and varied country. There are 316 other metro areas besides New York, Chicago, Philadelphia, and Detroit. Most metro areas would benefit substantially from metropolitan approaches.

Urban "Triage"

In effect, a national urban policy should approach metropolitanization as a type of urban "triage." The different stages might be called preventive medicine, out-patient treatment, major surgery, and life-support systems.

Preventive medicine would apply to most small metropolitan areas (fewer than 200,000 residents) where an urban core exists within a rural or semirural region. The most effective preventive medicine would be to merge immediately the core city and the surrounding county into a unified government. (Over 90 percent of the small metro areas are single-county areas.)

However, unifying city and county governments is not essential as long as the core city exercises broad annexation powers over urbanizing areas (including areas in adjacent counties). In addition, a core city should have the power to veto the incorporation of any competing new municipalities within a certain distance of its city limits.

In effect, preventive medicine inoculates against the emergence of fiscal disparities. It also tends to immunize a youthful metro area against the development of sharp jurisdictional schisms along racial and class lines.

Like all preventive medicine, inoculation and immunization would be relatively cheap. State legislatures must ensure that the right laws are on the books. Such laws should cover municipal annexation powers, conditions for municipal incorporation, and consolidation of local governments.

Most of the larger high- and hyper-elasticity metro areas should receive *out-patient treatment*. By no means are they ill now, but as they grow out of adolescence, they will become less resistant to the ills that come with maturity.

Maintaining the ability of high- and hyper-elasticity cities to grow through annexation is important. Increasingly, however, they are surrounded by independent suburbs that, like parasites, draw off their hosts' vigor. Parasitism can be combated through city-county consolidation. City-county consolidation is tough political medicine, but it can be self-administered locally, given the right prescription.

Low- and medium-elasticity areas are subtly infected with a still operable cancer: incipient central city decline amid suburban growth. Left untreated, the city-suburb schism will become fatal. The cancer, however, is so imbedded that it cannot be excised by purely local action. *Major surgery* is required by state government in the form of city-county consolidation or state mandates regarding areawide revenue sharing and areawide affordable housing strategies. The path to a complete cure is long and arduous, but a cure is achievable if the patient is in the hands of skilled professionals. Purely home remedies will not cure the ills of low- and medium-elasticity areas.

Zero-elasticity areas, in particular, cities past the point of no return, are candidates for *life-support systems*. Their disease is so far advanced that, for many, there is no long-term cure in any organic sense. Many of these cities are in highly complex, multicounty (or even multistate) metropolitan regions. Single-county consolidation would not have a dramatic impact on such a city's health, although it would be better than no action whatsoever. Yet forging multicounty metropolitan government would be extraordinarily difficult.

Life-support systems emphasize limited-in-scope policies that have some of the benefits of metro government, but do not require actual governmental reorganization. Such actions would include major state and federal urban aid programs targeted on cities suffering major fiscal disparities; state or federal guarantees of central city bonds to reduce financing costs; and state or county assumption of financing (and administering) certain central city programs.

Life-support systems are designed to keep zero-elasticity cities alive. They cannot make them well. For some zero-elasticity cities a miracle could happen—a political conversion that would clear away the seemingly insurmountable political barriers to drastic reform. Absent such a miracle, many zero-elasticity cities may die. With their death, their suburbs may wither away as well. Limbs cannot survive without the heart.

There is, however, one wonder drug that can overcome the central consequence of inelasticity for. inelastic cities: relieve them of the burden of being home to so many of their metro areas' poorest minority households. All communities in the whole region must shoulder the burden of minority poverty on a "fair share" basis. In highly complex, fragmented metropolitan areas, neither benefit sharing nor burden sharing happens voluntarily. In particular, the very thought that poor people (that is, poor Black or Hispanic people) should be integrated into middle-class neighborhoods traumatizes local politics. (A reminder: most poor Whites are already scattered in middle-class, generally suburban, neighborhoods.) Effective public action to open metropolitan societies to the integration of minority poor must flow from the federal and state governments.

Metro Government: A Definition

Before examining the mechanisms and politics of creating metro governments, I need to offer a working definition of what a metro government is. The country abounds with over 33,000 special purpose units of local government (transit authorities, water and sewer agencies, and community college districts, for exam-

ple). Often they are metrowide. Although creating special purpose governments may be a step toward ultimately achieving
metropolitan unification, a true metro government must be a
general purpose local government. It must have all of the powers of a municipality under applicable state law. Moreover, it
must exercise exclusive powers within its jurisdiction. In other
words, it must not be a general government that fills in the in-
terstices between on-going major municipal enclaves. This, un-
fortunately, is the situation of many county governments in
urban areas.

A metro government need not be responsible for all local public functions. Depending on local conditions, special purpose
and general governments can still exist, but a metro government
must control key planning and zoning powers. These decisions
must not be subject to veto by other local bodies.

Though preferable, a metro government need not cover the entire metro area; it should contain at least 60 percent of the area's
population. Moreover, a metro government must contain the region's central city (or a preponderance of multiple central cities).

I have categorized metro governments in three classes based
on the percentage of the metro area population that is served.
Class III serves between 60 percent and 74 percent of the metro
population. Class II serves between 75 percent and 99 percent of
the metro population. Class I serves 100 percent of the metro
population.[1]

State Government Initiatives

Although this book is written from Washington, D.C., it is based
on my experiences as a mayor and state legislator. Restructuring
local governance is not primarily a task for the federal government. It is primarily the responsibility of citizens and political
leaders at the local and state levels.

As I stated earlier, successfully challenging racial and class attitudes underlying the fragmentation of many metro areas is the
toughest political task in America. Rarely will a White county
commissioner or Black mayor champion actions to unify metro
areas (in more than a limited and voluntary way) *and* survive
local voter backlash (White or Black).

America, however, is a *federal system*. Within the bounds of
our national constitution, the states have sovereign powers. To

Box 3.1 An Inner-City–Inner-Suburb Coalition in the Minnesota Legislature

"Well, the Twin Cities are different," skeptics often scoff when I cite the area as a model of regional reform. And the Twin Cities area *is* different. It has a high level of civic culture, a twenty-seven-year old Metropolitan Council (Met Council), and a seven-county, 189-municipality "fiscal disparities plan"—the nation's most far-reaching regional revenue-sharing mechanism.

But what really distinguishes the area is that older, inner-ring, blue-collar suburbs are making common cause with the central cities. Primarily through the inspired efforts of Representative Myron Orfield of Minneapolis, legislators from such communities as Columbia Heights and Brooklyn Park now recognize that "inner city" problems, for example poverty, crime, and declining schools, are rising rapidly in their communities. Both older suburbs and central cities are being equally victimized by policies and practices channeling three-quarters of the region's growth into wealthy "fertile crescent" suburbs like Bloomington, Edina, and Eden Prairie.

As a result, legislators from the central cities, older suburbs, and Democrat-represented rural areas have formed a powerful legislative coalition. In the 1993 and 1994 sessions, the coalition passed strong metrowide "fair share" housing bills (both times vetoed by the Independent-Republican governor), restricted use of tax increment financing only for depressed communities, changed state tax laws to remove incentives to subdivide farmland, and placed three regional agencies controlling transportation planning, transit services, and sewer services under the Met Council. In 1995 the coalition added high-end residential property to the Regional tax base–sharing plan (another veto). Converting the Met Council from gubernatorial appointment to direct election failed by one vote.

The reform movement continues to broaden its base. Over 350 suburban churches have become members of the Alliance for Metropolitan Stability, an organization committed to "fair share" housing in the suburbs. Two dozen older suburbs have embraced the proposal for a metrowide, unified tax base. And support from the press, civic and business groups, and religious leadership continues to grow.

In regional reform the Twin Cities area is the school of America. The case can be made for building similar political coalitions between central cities and older suburbs in many other older metro areas. The facts are similar. What is missing is political leadership.

varying degrees, local governments (and local school districts) are legal subjects of state government. State legislatures frame the standards and procedures by which new municipalities are created. Typically, state governments do more than merely set the ground rules for local initiative. Most state legislatures can also create new local governments and merge old ones (including school districts)—often without a constitutional requirement for local voter approval.

Furthermore, governors and state legislators can and do act as metrowide policymakers. There are instances when state governments have mandated areawide local cooperation in a wide range of functional activities (transportation planning, sewage treatment, air quality control, senior citizens programs) or—much more rarely—areawide tax sharing or areawide affordable housing programs.

State government also plays an increasingly important role in revenue sharing for local government and, above all, for local school systems. By 1992 state aid had grown to 21 percent of city government revenues and 32 percent of county government revenues. By 1991 state governments were providing 45 percent of local school districts' budgets. With the purse comes additional power (and responsibility) to provide for the more rational and equitable organization of metro areas.

Statutory authority aside, however, why should state legislators and governors have any greater political opportunity to implement unpopular reforms? Are they not elected by the same voters as local officials?

Governors, of course, have statewide constituencies, and most state legislative districts are not coterminous with local government jurisdictions. Moreover, there is a tendency to view central cities and suburbs as monolithic blocks automatically opposed to each other. In reality there is tremendous variety among central cities (which I have tried to illustrate) and, above all, suburban communities. The variety among suburbs is the key to building effective political coalitions in state legislatures. Both inelastic central cities and older, often blue-collar, suburbs are victimized by typical metropolitan growth patterns that focus most high-end residential and commercial development in newer suburbs. Indeed, when "inner-city" problems begin to grow rapidly in older, blue-collar suburbs, these communities often have less resources available to combat rising poverty, crime, and other problems than central cities. Central cities and older suburbs are potentially allied by mutual self-interest, and the state legislature is the arena in which bonds can be forged, as is happening in the Minnesota legislature (see Box 3.1).

UNIFY LOCAL GOVERNMENTS

There are three different paths by which state legislatures can help create unitary metropolitan governments. In single-county metro areas, urban county governments can be fully empowered and municipal governments abolished; or county and municipal governments can be consolidated into new, unified governments. In multicounty metro areas, cities and existing counties can be combined into a single, regional government. Each of these three options will be discussed in turn.

Empowering urban counties.   Except in the Northeast and parts of the Midwest (see Box 3.2), counties have been the basic framework of local government within which municipalities (a more intensive form of local government) come into being. Counties typically predate urban development. They are the creation of a state or territorial legislature, which initially partitioned the state or territory's land into large governing units. County jurisdictions are remarkably stable. There are today 3,043 counties in the United States; forty years ago there were 3,052 counties. (Such stability has given rise to the adage that "the legislature may create municipalities, but only God can create a county.")

County government typically has been the principal government of rural and small-town America. As urbanization occurs, municipalities are formed to control development through planning and zoning and to provide a more intensive level of local services. Generally, county government continues to be responsible countywide (including within municipalities) for certain services—the county courts (state criminal trials), county assessor (property tax assessment), county treasurer (property tax collection), county clerk (records and elections), and often a county hospital (indigent health care). In addition, counties provide public services (roads, parks, fire and police protection) to unincorporated areas of the county.

Over the decades, however, as areas have urbanized around older cities, counties have been empowered by legislatures to provide many municipal-type services to unincorporated areas. Urban county governments often rival or exceed major city gov-

---

**Box 3.2 Northern Tier's Governance Further
Fragmented by Townships**

From Maine to North Dakota, a northern tier of twenty states
has an additional level of local government beyond counties and
municipalities—towns and townships—some 16,666 in all. In fact,
in almost all these states the map is completely divided among
townships and municipalities. There are essentially no "unincorporated areas" dependent on county government for general governmental services.

In New England, New Jersey, and Pennsylvania, townships
have relatively broad powers and perform functions similar to
municipalities. Midwestern townships historically have per-
formed more limited functions, but as urban sprawl spreads,
many formerly rural townships are increasingly expected to provide municipal-type services.

It was the Continental Congress under the Articles of Confed-
eration that legislated a system of townships for the Midwest. The
Northwest Ordinance of 1785 required that the Northwest Territories be surveyed and divided into townships each six miles
square. As the different territories (Ohio, Indiana, Michigan, etc.)
became states, their constitutions converted "congressional townships" into local units of government.

Whatever townships' value in civilizing the nineteenth-century
frontier, on the threshold of the twenty-first century the overall

---

ernments in size and scope. Moreover, although county government is often more limited in the array of taxes it can levy, its
tax base is much broader than that of municipal governments
within its boundaries. (County government bond ratings are typically one full level above bond ratings of inelastic central cities
located within them.)

County government, when developed to the greatest extent,
becomes a major deliverer of urban services, such as the government of Los Angeles County. County government may become the dominant local unit of government, both providing
services and controlling area development. Montgomery County,
Maryland, is an outstanding example (see Box 2.3).

The most direct—and probably most efficient—path to creating metropolitan government in the majority of metro areas is to
empower urban county government, have it absorb the functions
and responsibilities of all municipal governments within its

effect is the atomization of local government throughout the Northern Tier. In New England, balkanization is somewhat restrained. Connecticut, for example, has 169 towns and cities—an average of one local government for every 19,400 residents.

By comparison Pennsylvania, with 2,636 local general governments, has one for every 4,600 residents, and Minnesota, with 2,745 local general governments, has one for every 1,600 residents. Illinois, with 102 counties, 1,282 municipalities, and 1,433 townships (not to mention its 997 independent school districts and another 2,995 special districts), is the champion of microgovernment.

While most Midwestern cities retain some annexation powers over townships, it is common for townships to incorporate as independent municipalities in the face of pending annexation. And only the fact that townships in Indiana have, in effect, no governmental functions was the consolidation of Indianapolis and Marion County feasible.

The New England town meeting is enshrined in the American myth, and the National Association of Towns and Townships proudly proclaims itself the champion of "hometown government" and "grassroots government." The Northern Tier, however, embraces most of the most racially and economically segregated metro areas in the nation, and local communities' ability to compete economically is constantly constrained by the absence of governance structures to pull together regional resources.

boundaries, and abolish all municipalities. This is an action that is fully within the legal powers of most state legislatures even if at present such sweeping urban reorganization is beyond legislators' desires and political powers.

Consolidating cities and counties.   Typically, movements to create areawide governmental units have focused on consolidating municipal governments with their surrounding county governments. In recent decades the most notable consolidations have merged the central city with single counties. Indianapolis-Marion County, Nashville-Davidson County, and Jacksonville-Duval County are examples. (On the Indianapolis-Marion County consolidation, see Box 3.3; on the Nashville-Davidson County consolidation, see Box 3.4.)

Each city-county consolidation has been custom-made for its area. The ultimate structure represents a compromise with tra-

---

Box 3.3 Unigov Propels Indianapolis to Big League Status

On a wintry midnight in March 1983, big vans moved the NFL's Baltimore Colts to Indianapolis. This dark night will live in infamy for Baltimore civic boosters, but it announced to the world that Indianapolis had arrived in "the bigs."

The crucial step toward acquiring a pro football team was probably taken on January 1, 1970, when "Unigov" came into existence. The consolidation of the city of Indianapolis and Marion County by legislative act was the first to occur without a popular referendum since New York City was created in 1898.

Unigov happened because a visionary political leader, Indianapolis's young Republican mayor Richard Lugar (now a senator), seized the moment in 1968–69. For the first time in memory, Republicans controlled the mayor's office and city council, the county commission, the state legislature, and the governor's mansion. Through city-county consolidation, Lugar hoped to unite a fragmented governance structure behind the leadership of the mayor's office, reinvigorate the area's economic development efforts, and, by annexing tens of thousands of "suburban" voters, lock up control of Indianapolis city government for the Republican Party for decades to come.

Lugar's core group scoped out the basic consolidation plan. Then the mayor appointed a Task Force on Governmental Structure under the aegis of the business-based Greater Indianapolis Progress Committee. The task force of civic, business, and gov-

---

dition and political realities. Traditional functions of county government may be absorbed into the new, unified government (Nashville-Davidson) or continued as independent functions while the new government assumes service-providing functions for all unincorporated areas (Indianapolis-Marion County). Bowing to political reality, certain municipal enclaves may remain (for example, the town of Speedway within Indianapolis), and rural residents may have to be reassured through creation of lower service, lower tax zones (Nashville).

Despite such compromises, city-county consolidations do initially achieve the key goals: unification of the tax base and centralization of planning and zoning authority. With the continued spread of suburbia and long-distance commuting, the long-term dilemma is that metro areas often grow beyond the boundaries of the consolidated governments. Indianapolis-Marion County, ernmental leaders drafted an eighty-six-page bill modeled in part on the Nashville and Jacksonville consolidations. With business leadership out front, Lugar lobbied consolidation through the Republican-controlled legislature.

Unigov was something of a misnomer. Three small municipalities and separate hospital and airport authorities were left unconsolidated. A dozen county constitutional offices were continued, including the office of the Marion County sheriff. Public education was left in twenty-two separate school districts, bolstering more racial segregation than characterizes other consolidated communities. (Indeed, many in Indianapolis's Black community felt Unigov was designed to dilute the emerging voting power of Blacks.)

Consolidation, however, instantly re-energized Indianapolis, expanding its tax base and cementing a blue-chip municipal bond rating. Lugar's successor as mayor, William Hudnut, praises Unigov. "It brought better delivery of services and lower taxes—taxes that don't go up as fast. Equally important, consolidation has created a wider sense of community that helps you sell your city."[1] Selling their city, Unigov and the business community set out to promote Indianapolis into becoming a major, year-round sports venue.

New Year's Day, 1970. Baltimore should have "heard footsteps."

1. "Group Hears Indianapolis Mayor Laud Consolidation," *Albuquerque Journal*, March 2, 1991.

Nashville-Davidson County, and Jacksonville-Duval County were all highly successful consolidations of the 1960s. Today Indianapolis-Marion County is 59 percent of its ten-county metro area; Nashville-Davidson, 50 percent of its six-county area; and Jacksonville-Duval County, 70 percent of its five-county area. With the populations of outlying counties growing rapidly, metropolitanization must be updated.

Combining counties into regional governments.   The most significant multicounty combination is also the least remembered: the creation of New York City in 1898 (Box 1.2). Several independent local communities in what are now New York City's five boroughs were combined. For its first fifty years the consolidated result—New York City—functioned very well. Since the 1950s, however, the consequences of the White middle-class movement to the suburbs and the burgeoning low-income Black

---

Box 3.4 Consolidation Played Right Tune for Music City, USA

By the 1960s the city of Nashville's population was dropping, its downtown decaying, and many leading businesses were preparing to leave. Thirty years later Nashville-Davidson is the booming heart of a million-person region, the music industry capital of the country, and Tennessee's undisputed center of government, insurance, banking, and apparel manufacturing.

The turning point was the consolidation of Nashville with surrounding Davidson County—an action approved by the voters in 1962 although they had rejected another consolidation proposal four years earlier. In one step a city of 73 square miles and 170,000 people became a city of 473 square miles and 399,000 people. (Today Nashville has a population of 488,000.)

Beverly Briley, then county executive of Davidson County, led the successful campaign for consolidation over the opposition of Nashville's mayor and many entrenched city councillors. A decade later Mayor Briley had high praise for the new Metro. "Prior to consolidation, the business community was fed up. I believe there is a direct relation between Metro and the revitalization that downtown Nashville is experiencing."[1]

Metro brought about a complete consolidation of all municipal and county functions. "County" residents' fears of higher taxes were assuaged by charter provisions for two services districts: an urban services district (the old city) with higher services and higher taxes, and a general services district (countywide). Areas formerly in the county petitioned to be "annexed" into the urban services district.

1. Quoted in "Nashville Thrives on a County-City Merger," *Business Week* September 25, 1971, p. 133.

---

and Hispanic populations within the city have largely obscured New York City's earlier success as a consolidated, multicounty regional government.

CONSOLIDATION IMPACT

By whatever method achieved state by state, recasting urban government on a unified, single-county basis would create metropolitan governments in most urban areas. Today only 48 of 320 metropolitan areas are served by metro governments as I have defined them (see Table 3.1). Most are medium-size communi-

TABLE 3.1
CURRENT METRO GOVERNMENTS

Class of metro government	Number of metro areas	Population	Percentage of national population
III	32	5,818,158	2.3%
II	15	2,311,829	0.9
I	1	226,330	0.1
Totals	48	8,356,317	3.3

ties. Of the forty-eight—which are scattered among twenty-one states—the largest are San Antonio (935,933), Jacksonville (635,230), Memphis (610,337), El Paso (513,342), Tucson (405,390), and Albuquerque (384,736).

Fully empowering urban county government or consolidating central cities with home counties would revolutionize urban governance for most of the nation. As Table 3.2 shows, 256 metro areas could be served by metro government.

Sixty metro areas (including twenty-one of the forty-six metro areas of 1,000,000 or more residents) would not reach the minimum threshold for a metro government (that is, 60 percent) by single-county unification. New York, Philadelphia, Detroit, Washington, D.C., Boston, and Atlanta are in this category. More far-reaching measures would be needed for these areas to achieve greater metropolitan unity.

Conversely, many of the nation's biggest metro areas—among them, Chicago, Cleveland, Pittsburgh, Milwaukee, Buffalo, and Oakland—would be substantially unified. Included are zero-elasticity areas suffering from inner-city isolation as well as more elastic areas.

TABLE 3.2
POTENTIAL METRO GOVERNMENTS AFTER
SINGLE-COUNTY UNIFICATION

Class of metro government	Number of metro areas	Population	Percentage of national population
III	51	22,916,117	9.2%
II	46	24,381,322	9.8
I	158	57,057,701	23.0
Totals	256	104,355,140	42.0

TABLE 3.3
POTENTIAL UNIFICATION IMPACT AFTER
SINGLE-COUNTY UNIFICATION

Metro population	Number of metro areas	Number of metro governments	Percentage of metro areas with metro government
1.0 Million+	46	25	54%
.500-.999	46	37	80
.200-.499	93	79	85
.050-.199	130	119	92
Totals	315	260	83

Even more significant, however, countywide unification would metropolitanize most of the country's medium-size and smaller urban areas. Table 3.3 summarizes the effect by metro population size. For the remainder, achieving metropolitan government would require multicounty combinations.

City-county consolidation has been relatively rare—only twenty-one since World War II. In fact, only fourteen states have specific statutes authorizing city-county consolidation and setting forth the procedures for its achievement (see Table 3.4). Of the fourteen states, six are in the West, five in the South, three

TABLE 3.4
STATE LAWS REGARDING CITY-COUNTY CONSOLIDATION

	Number of states				
			Total		
State law	South (16)	West (13)	Midwest (12)	Northeast (9)	USA (50)
Consolidation of cities and counties is authorized	5	6	3	0	14
Referendum and majority approval of each city affected is required	1	3	2	0	6
Referendum and majority approval of county is required	4	3	0	0	7
Referendum and majority approval of unincorporated area of county is required	0	0	1	0	1

in the Midwest, and none in the Northeast, where counties often hardly exist as meaningful governmental units. Except for California, Indiana, Utah, and Virginia, all fourteen states require various forms of local referenda.

The absence of authorizing legislation, however, does not preclude most legislatures from enacting specific city-county consolidations as legislative acts. Such, indeed, was the path followed successfully in consolidating Indianapolis-Marion County as well as, a century ago, in creating New York City.

Uniform state laws should be enacted to encourage city-county consolidation through local initiative. The desirable provisions of such laws would include

1. establishing a consolidation charter commission by action of city or county government or both;
2. authorizing the creation of urban and rural service districts (with different tax levels) within a consolidated government;
3. authorizing the inclusion of traditional county functions (assessor, clerk, and so on) in the consolidated government; and
4. authorizing approval of the consolidated government by a single referendum of all affected voters (no single-jurisdiction veto).

Unifying local government in metro areas, however, is primarily a task for state government. There are too many obstacles at the local level, including entrenched officeholders, to rely on local initiative. For reforms to occur on a widespread scale, action must be taken by far-sighted and politically courageous governors and state legislators.

AUTHORIZE ANNEXATION

A second initiative needed by the states is to improve local annexation authority. For many small, relatively young metro areas, the central city's ability to annex urbanizing areas will be sufficient to maintain a basic unity of local government. Even in older, more built-up areas there are often opportunities for annexation that would benefit central cities. It is important to have good municipal annexation laws as tools to improve a city's elasticity.

Municipal annexation is authorized by general law in forty-four states (see Table 3.5). Once again, the Northeast lags: annex-

TABLE 3.5
STATE LAWS REGARDING MUNICIPAL ANNEXATIONS

State law	Number of states				
	South (16)	West (13)	Total Midwest (12)	Northeast (9)	USA (50)
Municipal annexation is authorized by state law	16	12	12	4	44
Initiated by property owner petition	12	10	9	3	34
Initiated by city ordinance or resolution	12	9	10	1	32
Public hearing is required	10	8	7	2	27
Referendum and majority approval in city are required	8	2	4	0	14
Referendum or majority approval in area to be annexed is required	11	3	3	2	19
Approval of county governing authority is required	1	6	4	0	11

ations are specifically authorized only (and only technically, at that) in Massachusetts, New Jersey, New York, and Pennsylvania.

Many states, however, attach conditions that can severely inhibit a municipality's ability to annex. Thirty-four states allow the annexation process to be initiated by a petition of property owners in the area to be annexed. Usually the support of a majority or extraordinary majority of property owners is required. In nine of these states, annexation can be initiated *only* by property owner petition—a very severe limitation placing a city's expansion at the mercy of suburban developers and residents. By contrast, thirty-two states allow annexation to be initiated by city ordinance or resolution.

In nineteen states a referendum or majority approval of property owners in the area to be annexed is required—another tough hurdle except where large blocs of land are owned by a handful of pro-annexation developers. In fourteen states voters in the annexing city must approve the annexation—an invitation to opposition from no-growth advocates or minority political activists fearing dilution of minority voting power.

In eleven states the affected county government must approve any municipal annexation. If the county fears loss of revenues, this could be a very significant obstacle to municipal expansion.

Faced with an expanding municipality, property owners should have rights. I believe, however, that state law should empower municipalities to initiate and carry out annexations while protecting property owners against any harm from such actions. State statutes should protect annexed property owners against increased taxes without commensurate increased services and unwarranted intrusion in rural lifestyles, absent significant urbanization. There should be a presumption, however, that annexation will serve the larger public interest.

In general terms, a model state annexation statute would

1. set forth the standards by which an annexation would be deemed to serve the general public interest;
2. authorize annexation to be initiated either by petition by landowners or resolution by city council;
3. require public hearings and due process;
4. authorize annexation to be consummated by council action alone; and
5. allow affected landowners the right of appeal to the state's District Court in the event landowners are aggrieved because the annexation was approved or rejected in violation of state standards.

LIMIT NEW MUNICIPALITIES

The ease or difficulty with which new municipalities are formed strongly affects the degree of fragmentation of urbanizing areas into multiple local governments. Virtually all states in the South, West, and Midwest set some limitations regarding minimum population, minimum area, or minimum ad valorem tax base (see Table 3.6). These limitations, however, tend to be modest. With the exception of New York, northeastern states are silent on the matter. In effect, the geopolitical map of New England, New Jersey, New York, and Pennsylvania is set in concrete.

Sixteen states require a minimum distance between the proposed and existing municipalities. (In New Mexico, for example, the distance is five miles.) In retrospect, perhaps this is the most useful requirement limiting the formation of new municipalities.

TABLE 3.6
STATE LAWS REGARDING FORMING NEW MUNICIPALITIES

| | Number of states | | | | |
	South (16)	West (13)	Total Midwest (12)	Northeast (9)	USA (50)
State law					
Limits are imposed on incorporation of new local government units	15	12	12	1	40
Minimum population is required	14	12	9	1	36
Minimum area is required	5	4	7	1	17
Minimum distance from existing units is required	8	3	5	0	16
Minimum ad valorem tax base is required	0	3	3	0	6

Requirements regarding minimum population, minimum area, and minimum ad valorem tax base should be considerably higher than prevailing standards. (In general, I believe in strengthening county government rather than proliferating the number of towns and small cities.) State law also ought to provide for a substantial zone around existing municipalities in which the existing government can veto the incorporation of new municipalities or other public bodies.

Finally, there ought to be different classes of municipalities based on size of population. Large cities ought to be given the presumptive authority over smaller cities to annex contested lands or even to absorb smaller cities in quasi-consolidation-type actions. Small municipalities, in turn, should be able to appeal such actions by large municipalities to the state's District Court.

PROMOTE REGIONAL PARTNERSHIPS

The fourth state-based initiative I want to discuss is promoting regional partnerships. Short of reshaping the local political map, states can authorize or pursue functional policies to achieve some of the benefits of metro government. Forty-two states specifically authorize local governments to enter into joint powers or joint service agreements. These agreements allow local governments to band together to address problems that transcend local political boundaries. For the most part, joint powers or joint service agreements address infrastructure issues (for example, sewage treatment and air quality management) or "non-threatening" service needs (for example, emergency medical services and services for senior citizens). They rarely touch the core of social and economic divisions within metro areas—housing, schools, and fiscal disparities.

There are creative exceptions, however. Minneapolis–St. Paul has a multicounty tax-sharing compact (see Box 3.5). In the Portland, Oregon, area, the state legislature and area voters have created a unique metro government (see Box 3.6). With its own elected officials and independent taxing powers, this multiprogram government handles both a variety of infrastructure services and areawide land-use planning. The state legislature in Connecticut has recently enacted requirements for suburban governments to participate in affordable housing programs (see Box 3.7).

Woodrow Wilson called the states "the laboratory of democracy." America's urban problem presents the states with their toughest challenge to live up to that honored billing.

Federal Government Initiatives

In any constitutional sense the federal government has no role in the way in which local governments are organized within the states. The Congress cannot, for example, just legislate the organization of metropolitan governments. Federal policy, nevertheless, has had a decisive impact on the emergence of suburban America since World War II and on the corresponding decline of central cities.

- The Federal Housing Administration and the Veterans Administration have backed millions of low-interest mortgages for single-family homes in suburbia. Today the federal government's mortgage portfolio covers over 8 million homeowners—about 20 percent of all homes—with an outstanding principal of $400 billion.
- The U.S. Department of Transportation has made the auto-based suburbs possible. It has spent about $310 billion in federal aid for roads and highways (about half in urban areas). This has been about five times the amount of city-oriented federal aid for mass transit.
- The federal treasury forgoes $51 billion a year in tax revenues because mortgage interest (on homes largely in the suburbs) is

---

**Box 3.5 Tax-Base Sharing in the Twin Cities
Reduces Fiscal Disparities**

There has been only one significant experiment in the nation in metropolitan tax-base sharing. This is the fiscal disparities plan enacted by the Minnesota legislature in 1971.

The Twin Cities' Metropolitan Council thus describes the rationale for the Minneapolis-St. Paul plan:

> From a regional perspective the Twin Cities is one economy. Large commercial-industrial developments tend to concentrate in a few locations, drawing workers and clients from a market area that is larger than the city it is located in. Access to these concentrations, primarily highways, is a prime determinant of where these developments locate. Cities with such access are the ones most likely to get commercial-industrial development.
>
> Since the property tax is the primary source of local government revenues, certain types of development—office space, headquarters buildings, up-scale housing—are attractive because they typically generate more revenue than it costs to serve them. Not all cities can expect to attract such development, but most participate in financing the regional facilities serving these developments. The idea underlying tax-base sharing is to allow all cities to share in the commercial-industrial development that is, to a large extent, the result of the regional market and public investments made at the regional and state levels.[1]

Under the state law, the plan applies to 187 municipalities in the seven-county Twin Cities area. Since 1971, 40 percent of the *increase* in commercial-industrial property valuation has been placed in a common pool. (A city's pre-1971 assessed valuation is

---

deductible. By comparison, federal tax law provides only $1 billion a year in tax credits to encourage city-oriented, moderate-income apartment construction.

Even in an era of ever-shrinking federal aid, federal policy continues to promote urban sprawl—and the resultant decline of inelastic central cities. In effect, for fifty years the federal government's "national urban policy" has been a "national *suburban* policy."

If, as I believe, the "action" is really with state and local governments—and with citizens as state and local voters—what can exempted.) The pool is then taxed at a uniform rate and redistributed among all 188 municipalities based on annual estimated population and how each city's per capita market value of commercial-industrial property compares with the metrowide per capita value.

By 1995 the annual "fiscal disparities" fund amounted to $241 million, almost 27 percent of the region's $906 million in commercial-industrial assessed property valuation. Some 140 municipalities were net recipients; 47 were net contributors. The net contributors were primarily Twin Cities' major suburbs. Giant shopping malls, office towers, and garden-like industrial parks have sprouted along the interstate highways that cut through these suburbs or are adjacent to the suburban Minneapolis-St. Paul International Airport.

Initially the largest net recipient, Minneapolis became a large net contributor in the 1980s. This transformation was fueled by the office boom downtown. Minneapolis's $19 million net contribution in 1991 represented 6.5 percent of its commercial-industrial tax capacity. By 1995, however, office space devaluation made Minneapolis a net recipient again.

The tax-base sharing program is successfully reducing fiscal disparities between rich and poor communities. Among communities of 3,000 or more households the ratio of richest community to poorest community would be 17 to 1, as measured by per capita commercial-industrial property value. The pioneering "fiscal disparities" program has reduced the ratio to 4 to 1.

1. This quotation and all data are from Metropolitan Council, Minneapolis, Minnesota, *Fiscal Disparities Discussion Paper* (April 16, 1991).

the federal government do to stimulate movement toward metropolitan government? And perhaps more to the point, how can the federal government reform its own policies and conduct to give inelastic central cities—and their poor minority residents—if not preferential advantages, then at least an even break?

There are four critical areas that require federal action: providing incentives for metropolitan reorganization, amending requirements on federal infrastructure grants to slow urban sprawl, changing other anti-city federal policies, and ending the traditional federal public housing program.

Box 3.6 Portland's Unique Metro Government

We, the people of the Portland area metropolitan services district, in order to establish an elected, visible and accountable regional government that is responsive to the citizens of the region and works cooperatively with our local governments; that undertakes, as its most important services, planning and policy making to preserve and enhance the quality of life and the environment for ourselves and future generations; and that provides regional services needed and desired by the citizens in an efficient and effective manner, do ordain this charter for the Portland area metropolitan services district, to be known as Metro.

With that preamble, Portland area voters on November 3, 1992, adopted a "home rule" charter for the Portland Metropolitan Services District, established by the legislature in 1970. This vote in 1992 was the most recent step in the evolution of a unique approach to metro government in the Portland area—now three counties and twenty-four municipalities.

Metrowide special units of government are common. Portland's Metro is uncommon in the wide scope of its functions: solid waste collection, recycling, and disposal; transportation planning and allocation of federal highway and road funds; regional air and water quality programs; operation of the regional zoo; and construction and operation of the $85 million Oregon Convention Center. Metro also is unique because it is the only directly elected regional government in the United States. Under the guidance of its elected, seven-member, nonpartisan commission and elected executive officer, it has a $225 million annual budget and 1,200 employees.

In the new charter the area's citizenry affirmed that regional planning is Metro's "primary function." The charter charges Metro with developing a fifty-year "Future Vision" and a "Regional Framework Plan." The charter then empowers the Metro Council to adopt ordinances to require local comprehensive plans and zoning regulations to comply with the Regional Framework Plan, to adjudicate inconsistencies between regional and local plans, and to change inconsistent local land use standards and procedures. Metro also is empowered to carry out any other functions or services assigned to it by the state legislature or approved by the voters of the Metro district.

After decades of patient development, Portland's Metro is a model structure for multicounty regional governance.

INCENTIVES FOR METROPOLITAN REORGANIZATION

"Incentives" is a euphemism for federal money—either dollars spent or taxes not paid. Re-energizing the American economy, controlling health-care costs, and systematically reducing the federal deficit (including reforming Social Security) must be the paramount federal goals. Proposing incentives to promote metropolitan government is politically hazardous and intellectually troubling. I am certainly prepared to see metropolitan government advocated at state and local levels without federal incentives as long as the federal government stops doing active harm to the cause.

Nevertheless, I believe that the urban problem is central to our declining economic competitiveness. For America to revive its economic and social health, solving the urban problem is an essential component. Placing local governments on a sound financial basis, reducing racial and economic segregation, invigorating areawide economic growth, slowing urban sprawl—these are outcomes for which it is worth considering federal incentives.

In the first edition of *Cities without Suburbs*, I proposed a series of incentives from the federal government that would reward local citizens and communities for forming metro governments. I proposed increasing the federal income tax deduction allowed for local taxes paid to metro governments, boosting the tax credit allowed for purchasing bonds issued by metro governments, and adding bonuses to grant-in-aid allocations (except Medicaid) received by metro governments. The fiscal impact would have ranged from *zero* dollars (if no new metro governance arrangements were formed) to an estimated $23.5 billion (if all central cities, for example, were to consolidate with their central county). Whereas $23 billion is a lot of money (it is twice the level of annual federal farm subsidies), it would have been a small price to pay for the benefits.

Three years later, despite the significant budget reduction plan adopted in 1993 and again by the now Republican-majority Congress in 1995, the federal deficit is still untamed. With or without the Republican congressional takeover, the federal government clearly cannot afford to put major new money on the table for any domestic purpose.

So let me suggest how four decades of our national suburban policy can be amended to reverse the trends toward fragmentation of governance, urban sprawl, and growing racial and economic isolation of inner-city residents *without* requiring new money.

Encouraging formation of metro governments through tax policy.   Taxpayers now can deduct 100 percent of state and local income taxes and property taxes from federal taxable income. The deductions apply regardless of how fragmented, overlapping, duplicative, and wasteful the system of local governance is or how much fragmented local governance fosters racial and economic segregation and high fiscal disparities among local communities.

First, to help balance the federal budget, Congress could reduce the allowable federal income tax deduction to 50 percent of actual state and local income taxes and property taxes paid. Then, to encourage state and local initiatives for metropolitan governance, Congress could partially restore the cut as a "bonus" deduction for taxes paid by citizens to support metro governments.

For example, for actual taxes paid to a Class III metro government, taxpayers could be allowed to deduct 75 percent rather than 50 percent; to Class II, a 90-percent deduction; and to Class I, a 100-percent deduction. Thus, if a taxpayer currently pays $1,000 in municipal taxes, if the city consolidated with its county (achieving, say, Class I metro government status), the taxpayer could deduct not $500 (under the federal tax code revisions I propose), but $1,000 (the actual amount he or she paid). The result would be a savings to the federal taxpayer of $140 on his or her current tax bill (an additional $500 deduction multiplied by a 28-percent marginal tax rate).

Furthermore, if the new consolidated government were to seek the taxpayer's support for a $200 tax increase, the real cost to the taxpayer would be only $144. The other $56 would be recaptured by the taxpayer in federal taxes not paid ($200 times 28 percent equals $56).

There are two economic objections to this proposal that are also political strengths. First, deducting state and local taxes is highly regressive since only about 20 percent of all federal taxpayers (generally from higher income groups) itemize their deductions. These are precisely the taxpayers—often upper-income suburbanites—whose support for metro government must be encouraged.

Second, levels of state and local taxation differ among the states. New York, for example, is a high-tax state; Texas is a low-

TABLE 3.7
RECAPTURE OF $20.5 BILLION IN TAX DEDUCTIONS
BY RESIDENTS OF CURRENT METRO GOVERNMENTS

Class of metro governments	Number of metro governments	Population percentage	Bonus deduction rate	Value of bonus deduction
				(in millions of dollars)
III	32	2.3%	50%	$235.8
II	15	0.9	80	147.6
I	1	0.1	100	20.5
Totals	48	3.3	N/A	403.9

tax state. Thus, federal rewards for metropolitanization might flow proportionally more to New Yorkers than to Texans. However, city-county consolidation would be achieved more easily in Texas than in New York because of Texas's larger-sized counties, more dominant central cities, fewer suburban governments, and lower city-suburb racial gradients. In effect, residents of the Syracuse, Rochester, and Buffalo areas for example, would be rewarded more because achieving metropolitanization would have been more difficult than in Houston or Dallas or San Antonio.

Of course, reducing federal taxpayers' allowable deduction from the current 100-percent level to 50 percent of state and local taxes paid would surely be criticized as a federal income tax increase. And, without any bonuses for metropolitanization, the result would be a $20 billion tax increase (based on FY1996 estimates). However, in the 1986 Tax Reform Act Congress phased out deductibility of consumer interest payments (except for mortgage interest). Congress's judgment was that federal tax policy had encouraged too much consumer debt. Regarding my proposals, the congressional judgment would be that federal tax policy was rewarding highly fragmented governance—and societies highly segmented by income class and race.

Though almost 78 percent of the country's population lives in metro areas, reducing the state and local tax deduction to 50 percent would have to apply to taxpayers in nonmetropolitan areas as well. If rural taxpayers were able to deduct 100 percent of state and local taxes, urban sprawl would accelerate. More and more suburbanites would be encouraged to become *exurbanites,*

TABLE 3.8

RECAPTURE OF $20.5 BILLION IN TAX DEDUCTIONS BY RESIDENTS
OF POTENTIAL METRO GOVERNMENTS IF ALL CITY-SINGLE
COUNTY UNIFICATIONS OCCUR

Class of metro governments	Number of metro governments	Population percentage	Bonus deduction rate	Value of bonus deduction
				(in millions of dollars)
III	51	9.2%	50%	$ 943.0
II	46	9.8	80	1,607.2
I	158	23.0	100	4,715.1
Totals	256	42.0%	N/A	7,265.2

living on the far edges of metro areas' commuting range. Thus, my proposals would seem to unfairly penalize rural residents for an urban problem by reducing their federal income tax deductions along with that of urban taxpayers.

Yet in rural areas the path to restoring 100-percent deductibility of state and local taxes would be readily available: empower county governments as the local general governments. This act would not require abolition of municipalities and townships as service deliverers, but county governments would have to exercise overall taxation and land use controls.

Setting aside the rural issue, what would be the fiscal impact of these proposals? As the preceding estimate shows, halving deductibility of state and local taxes would generate another $20.5 billion toward reducing the federal deficit. However, taxpayers representing 3.3 percent of the total population presently are served by what I have defined as forty-eight metro governments. Table 3.7 shows the estimated benefits that taxpayers in those forty-eight communities would receive from being allowed to claim higher deductions for state and local taxes paid.

In short, in the forty-eight metro governments that now exist, residents would pay $404 million less in federal taxes based on taxes they currently pay to their states and metro governments. Some $20.1 billion in increased taxes would be available for federal deficit reduction.

Furthermore, what would be the result if all central cities consolidated with their surrounding counties as illustrated in Table 3.2. The effect is estimated in Table 3.8.

About 42 percent of the nation's taxpayers—residents of areas with metro governments—would pay $7,265.2 billion less in federal taxes, leaving tax increases of over $13 billion to apply to the federal deficit. That amount would shrink further to the degree that states devised structures for regional governance in larger, multicounty metro areas, and rural areas adopted countywide governance.

Many metro areas are not currently in trouble. Should their citizens be rewarded for fixing something that "ain't broke"? The answer is yes. Preventive medicine is the cheapest policy in the long run. All areas, including nonproblem communities, should be encouraged to put their governmental houses in order.

SLOWING URBAN SPRAWL

Federal grant-in-aid programs for large public works pay a big portion of the bill for urban sprawl. Federal highway funds ($17.8 billion in FY1994) and sewage treatment grants ($2.1 billion in FY1993) have had the greatest impact. With the federal share varying from 75 percent to 90 percent, financing major sprawl-oriented infrastructure has been virtually free for state and local governments. Perhaps the most decisive antisprawl action would be for the federal budget balancers to end completely highway, sewage treatment, and other infrastructure grants. However, early evidence is showing that the Republican 104th Congress has less problem chopping "pork" for central cities (like federal subsidies for city bus and subway systems) than slicing into "essential federal aid" for suburbs. So let's talk about modifying how and why the federal government could subsidize future infrastructure projects.

Congress should amend the federal construction grants to require state and local government applicants to analyze the impact of each project on the metropolitan area's residential density (using densities from the 1990 census as the baseline). A sliding scale for federal participation would be established for each grant-in-aid program. For example, if a proposed widening of an urban-aid highway reaching out to the metropolitan periphery would promote more sprawl and new residential development at densities 50 percent below the region's average residential density, federal participation would be reduced from 75 percent of total project costs to 25 percent. Conversely, if applying for federal funds to build a light rail line that would encourage new

Box. 3.7 Connecticut Legislature
Champions Affordable Housing

In per capita income Connecticut is the country's wealthiest state. Its metro areas, however, rank ninth in racial segregation and first in economic segregation. Connecticut's housing patterns are partly to blame. Its central cities have been dominated by rental properties. (Hartford's residents, for example, are 80 percent renters.) Suburban towns have been oriented toward owner-occupied homes at towering prices.

High housing costs have had undeniable negative consequences. Many public employees (police officers, firefighters, teachers) cannot afford to live in the communities they serve. And many children cannot afford to live in the communities where they were raised.

As a result, the Connecticut General Assembly has passed a package of initiatives to stimulate more affordable housing.

To counter exclusionary zoning, the legislature explicitly authorized towns to adopt "inclusionary zoning" practices. For example, "density bonuses" allow developers to build more housing units per acre than local zoning would normally allow if they also build some affordable units.

To put enforcement teeth behind this policy, the General Assembly enacted in 1989 the Affordable Housing Land-Use Appeals Procedure. Under the new procedure, if a town rejects a developer's affordable housing proposal, the developer can challenge the local ruling in state court. The burden of proof would be on the town to prove that its reasons for rejecting the project "clearly outweigh the need for affordable housing." In effect, the legislature established the area's need for affordable housing as the primary public interest to be served and shifted the burden of proof from developer to town planning commission.

development at 25 percent above the region's average residential density, federal participation would increase from 75 percent to 90 percent.

The underlying principle is simple: if state and local governments want more urban sprawl, they should finance the lion's share of the costs themselves through increased state and local taxes and users fees.

Although suits can originate from communities throughout the state, appeals can be heard only by the state superior court in Hartford-New Britain. The legislation urged that cases be assigned to a "small number of judges so that a consistent body of expertise can be developed." The first two dozen appeals were all heard by the two judges—with findings in over half the cases supporting the affordable housing proposal.

Connecticut's law is not going to produce affordable housing on every village lane. First, the income ceiling for buying or renting affordable housing is set at 80 percent of an area's median income (about $29,000 for a four-person family statewide in 1990). Mortgage payments or monthly rentals cannot exceed 30 percent of family income. Second, a developer's project proposal can qualify if as little as 20 percent of the units are priced as affordable housing. Finally, communities where "assisted housing" already exceeds 10 percent of the housing supply are exempted. (Only about 25 of Connecticut's 169 towns meet or exceed this standard.) Also exempted are communities actively participating in Connecticut's Housing Partnership Program or Regional Fair Housing Compact Pilot Program.

Despite these qualifications, the Affordable Housing Land-Use Appeals Procedure should encourage racial and economic integration in Connecticut. As a Connecticut attorney notes, "The unequal distribution of wealth and resources caused in part by towns' exclusionary land use decisions . . . created an imbalance between the housing needs of low-income, urban minorities and the housing opportunities of their more affluent, white, suburban neighbors. Opening up the suburbs to the full range of economic classes will . . . promote racial dispersal."[1]

1. Quoted in Melinda Westbrook, "Connecticut's New Affordable Housing Appeals Procedure Assaulting the Presumptive Validity of Land Use Decisions," *Connecticut Bar Journal* (June 1992). Other information cited in this box has been drawn from this source.

Leveling the Playing Field

Federal housing finance programs, environmental regulations, and tax laws are riddled with provisions that tilt the playing field in favor of newer suburban areas and against central cities and older suburbs. For example, the Environmental Protection Agency's stringent rules regarding the cleanup of abandoned industrial sites make pristine suburban "greenfields" much cheaper to develop than urban "brownfields." The "brownfields" issue has been targeted by mayors of many older, industrial cities as crying for sensible reforms.

One of the most subtle anti-city/anti-older suburb policies is the federal tax code treatment of capital gains realized from the sale of homes. Current federal law taxes the capital gain on home sale unless the seller buys a new home of equal or greater value within two years of the sale. After age fifty-five, a homeowner has a one-time capital gains exemption of $125,000.

In many metro areas home values grow in almost concentric rings away from the urban core because postwar developers are constantly building the newest and best homes farther and farther out. Studying Ohio's seven major metro areas, Tom Bier of Cleveland State University found that about 85 percent of homesellers who step up in price also step out geographically; only about 15 percent move closer in.[2] By contrast, about 35 percent of homesellers who subsequently buy lower-priced houses or become renters move closer in. The capital gains tax adds to the abandonment of older city neighborhoods and older, inner suburbs. [3]

Rather than include home sales as part of the partisan debate on overall capital gains taxation, Congress should eliminate entirely capital gains taxation on the sale of homes. This step would be good urban policy, good environmental policy, and good fiscal policy.

In many metro areas, repeal of the capital gains tax would boost demand for central city/older suburban housing. Removing an obstacle in the way of homeowners' buying down or becoming renters would enhance the incentive to move closer in, ease development pressures on the periphery, and strengthen the use of existing neighborhoods and infrastructure. This change could do far more to revitalize older, distressed communities than could empowerment and enterprise zones. In addition, repeal would slow the urban sprawl that is gobbling up agricultural land voraciously.

The federal treasury collects only about $2.6 billion a year from capital gains tax on home sales because four out of five homesellers reinvest any gain in a new house of equal or greater value. *In short, the impact of capital gains tax on homeseller/homebuyer conduct is many times greater than its actual impact on federal revenues.*

The revenue loss might be readily made up by lowering the ceiling on the maximum mortgage principal eligible for interest deduction. The mortgage ceiling is currently $1 million. If the ceiling were lowered to $300,000 (which would still cover over 96 percent of all mortgages), it would yield $4.5 billion in new revenues, more than offsetting the $2.6 billion lost from repealing homeowners' capital gains liability.

ENDING PUBLIC HOUSING PROJECTS

In the first edition of *Cities without Suburbs,* I added my voice to the many that were calling for radical overhaul of the federal public housing program. "Housing the urban poor in high-density, inner-city public housing projects is patently destructive and should be ended as soon as possible," I wrote. "The federal court-ordered Gautreaux Project in the Chicago area has demonstrated the striking effectiveness of metrowide [rent subsidies]. . . . The federal government should adopt a Gautreaux-type strategy for public housing on a nationwide scale."

Three years later, with the vigorous advocacy of Housing and Urban Development (HUD) Secretary Henry Cisneros, the Clinton administration's policy proposals have pushed beyond even what I had envisioned. On December 20, 1994, Secretary Cisneros proposed to "totally transform public housing" as part of HUD's "Reinvention Blueprint."

"Public housing projects have become traps for the poorest of the poor rather than a launching pad for families trying to improve their lives," Cisneros stated in announcing HUD's plans. Over a three-year transition period, HUD planned to convert all project-based public housing subsidies into tenant-based rental assistance. During FY1996 and FY1997, HUD would deregulate more than 3,000 well-performing local housing authorities, work to reform more than 100 severely troubled authorities, and divest ten to fifteen of the most troubled local authorities beyond any reasonable hope of property improvement and management control. During FY1996 HUD would consolidate all public housing funds into a capital fund and operating subsidies fund. States and localities could opt to receive all housing funds as housing certificates. By FY1998 all former project-based public housing subsidies would be completely portable housing certificates awarded to eligible low-income households. Owned and operated by housing authorities, the projects would have to compete for the business of eligible low-income households, who would be able to use their vouchers for any rental properties throughout metro areas.

Inner-city slums, anchored by large public housing projects, must not simply be replaced by suburban slums, filled with poor households using their vouchers to rent hand-me-down houses or cheap private apartments built for the voucher market. The goal is to assimilate low-income households into standard housing in predominantly middle-class communities. Therefore, federal regulations are essential to prevent too many poor households from reconcentrating in older suburban areas. For example, federal regulations might not allow voucher use to exceed one-third of all rental units in an apartment building or might limit voucher use to neighborhoods where the poverty rate is less than 150 percent of the area's poverty rate. (That is, if the metropolitan poverty rate is 10 percent, vouchers could not be used in census tracts with a poverty rate of more than 15 percent.)

Does sufficient affordable housing exist in suburban areas to assimilate relocatees from inner-city housing markets? Certainly a substantial amount exists; after all, most poor whites live in suburban neighborhoods. And there are a few communities that have voluntarily mandated mixed-income housing development, such as Montgomery County, Maryland (see Box 2.3).

Here again, a shift in federal policy can help. After decades of allowing, even fostering red-lining of inner-city neighborhoods, the federal government is redirecting private mortgage funds toward inner-city areas. The Community Reinvestment Act (CRA) requires mortgage lenders to meet new targets for mortgage and renovation loans in older neighborhoods. The federally chartered secondary mortgage market agencies like Fannie Mae and Freddie Mac must ensure that 20 percent of lending they back occurs in central cities.

Overall, such requirements have helped level the playing field. However, it is ironic that sometimes meeting CRA goals have resulted in mortgage lenders helping build low-income housing projects precisely where they should not be built: in poverty-impacted, inner-city neighborhoods. The CRA and other federal regulations should be amended to allow mixed-income housing, accessible to former public housing tenants, in suburban areas to meet federal goals as well.

This four-part federal agenda is based on two principles. First, echoing the old Hippocratic oath, "do no more harm." Second, echoing the apparent message of the 1994 congressional elections, "spend no more money." If the federal government truly reformed the way it does business in urban America as outlined in the preceding paragraphs, states and local governments would be motivated to change substantially the way they approach urban issues.

The federal government can provide intellectual leadership, spurring growing national recognition of the need to reorganize local government to address regional issues. HUD could turn its research agenda toward city-suburb relations and the other issues raised by my analysis.

There are other possibilities for helpful federal initiatives. During the 1970s the U.S. Advisory Commission on Intergovernmental Relations (ACIR) was a constant source of provocative recommendations affecting the federal-state-local system. During the conservative decade of the 1980s, however, the ACIR eschewed practically any involvement in the complex cauldron of racial and class issues shaping urban America. A revitalized ACIR could play a key role in focusing renewed attention on metropolitan disparities and intergovernmental reform.

The best public policy "bully pulpit" is the White House. President Bill Clinton has numerous meetings with delegations of mayors petitioning Uncle Sam for help. And responds as much as the head of a debt-ridden government can respond. But he needs to promote new ways of thinking about old problems. What would be the effect of the president responding to the mayors something like this:

> Well, mayors, I want to assure you that my administration will do all we can to help. But let me ask you a question. Your cities sit in the middle of some of the wealthiest urban areas in the country. What can you do to get more help from your neighbors and start solving some of these problems without relying so much on Washington? Why don't you think about that some and come back to me with a plan.

Of course, most big city mayors do not have the power to achieve such solutions on their own. But most are not even thinking along these lines.

Prodding such thinking is cheap for a president. It costs the federal treasury nothing. It may cost the president some initial political capital. But capital hoarded is valueless. It must be invested to be productive. No American president since Lyndon Johnson has seriously invested presidential capital in pushing this nation to deal with the roots of inequality.

Box 3.8 Ice Tea: The Fed's New Regional Brew

After languishing at the federal level throughout the 1980s, regionalism was revived in 1991 when Congress passed the Intermodal Surface Transportation Efficiency Act (ISTEA).

Since 1973 local governments have been involved in planning the use of certain federal funds for transportation. In the judgment of the National Association of Regional Councils, ISTEA "marks a radical and visionary transformation in the nation's transportation policy."[1]

ISTEA authorizes $151 billion over six years (fiscal years 1992-97) for highway and transit assistance. The key change is the greater discretion afforded local officials in the use of federal funds.

In the past local planning was largely limited to prioritizing laundry lists of projects within narrow, federally prescribed program allocations. Under ISTEA, "Metropolitan Planning Organizations" (MPOs) for all urbanized areas with 200,000 or more residents will have broad discretion to allocate lump-sum federal funds among road, bridge, and transit projects.

About half of all MPOs are "regional councils," voluntary consortia of local governments with a variety of program interests beyond transportation planning. Other MPOs are regional economic development organizations, transportation planning agencies, and arms of state highway departments.

"ISTEA's implementation must not degenerate into a turf war-states, MPOs, and local governments all seeking primacy," warns the National Association of Regional Councils. "We must develop true collaborative approaches to planning and programming these funds."[2]

Transportation networks help determine how and where people live, work, and play. Yet transportation planning rarely excites passions (except, of course, when a new highway is planned through existing neighborhoods). ISTEA is an important building block toward greater regional integration.

1. National Association of Regional Councils, *Regional Reporter* 3 (January 1992):1

2. National Association of Regional Councils, "ISTEA of 1991: A Strategic Overview." Memorandum [1992]:1–2.

Box 3.9 From Failure in the Ghetto to Success in the Suburbs

The Gautreaux Project has drawn national attention by demonstrating that public housing tenants in inner cities can succeed simply by getting out of bad neighborhoods into better neighborhoods. Named for public-housing tenant activist Dorothy Gautreaux, the program began in 1976 when the federal courts found the Chicago Housing Authority (CHA) guilty of racial discrimination. One remedy the courts ordered was to subsidize moving public housing families out of CHA projects and into private rental housing elsewhere in Chicago or anywhere in Chicago's six-county suburban area.

Since 1976 over 5,600 families have participated in the program, administered by the Leadership Council for Metropolitan Open Communities, a court-appointed nonprofit organization. One-third of the families remained in Chicago; two-thirds moved to Chicago's suburbs.

James E. Rosenbaum, professor of sociology at Northwestern University, did a follow-up study of the "city movers" and "suburban movers."[1] Both showed the same socioeconomic profile entering the program: typically a Black, female head of household, receiving welfare assistance, with two or three children. Of the suburban-mover mothers, 64 percent were working compared with 51 percent for city-mover mothers. Of the suburban-mover children, 95 percent graduated from their suburban systems compared with a graduation rate of 80 percent of city movers from Chicago schools. Fifty-four percent of suburban movers had continued their education (27 percent in four-year colleges) compared with 21 percent of city movers (4 percent in four-year colleges). Seventy-five percent of suburban-mover youth were working (21 percent for hourly wages of $6.50 or better); by contrast, 41 percent of city-mover youth had a job (5 percent at $6.50 or better per hour).

"Pessimistic predictions of 'culture of poverty' models are not supported," Rosenbaum concluded after completing his study. "The early experiences of low-income blacks do not prevent them from benefitting from suburban moves."

One participant in the Gautreaux Project summed up her experience in this way: "A housing project deteriorates you. You don't want to do anything. Living in the suburbs made me feel that I'm worth something. I can do anything I want to do if I get up and try it."

1. James E. Rosenbaum, "Black Pioneers—Do Their Moves to the Suburbs Increase Economic Opportunity for Mothers and Children?" in Federal National Mortgage Association (Fannie Mae), *Housing Policy Debate*, 2: 1213.

Outcomes for both suburban movers and city stayers were presumably superior to those for households remaining in many of Chicago's high-rise public housing projects.

Citizen Initiatives

Brainstorming about federal initiatives is very seductive. It can lead readers (and authors) astray. Reorganizing local government is primarily a task for initiative and hard work at state and local levels.

Wherever major structural reforms have been accomplished, there has been a civic movement at the core of the effort. Typically such movements have been broad-based coalitions of citizens concerned about improving government from across the metro area, leading business and labor interests, civic organizations, and (less frequently) key local political leaders. In each of my case studies of city-county consolidation, such a metrowide coalition has played a vital role, whether the arena for change has been the state legislature or the ballot box.

A national leader in promoting voluntary civic action has been the National Civic League. Founded in 1894, the National Civic League helped nurture the so-called good government movement in the early decades of this century. Out of citizen reform coalitions in many communities arose sweeping changes in local government in many states, including adoption of the commission-manager system by many local governments and the evolution of career civil service systems.

For more than sixty years regional governance has been a focus of the National Civic League. In recent years the National Civic League has supported the emergence of what have been called "regional civic organizations." Their advantages are many, a National Civic League memo has noted.

> ...[W]hereas various attempts to expand regional government—for example, through city-county consolidations, annexations, and federations—have succeeded with declining frequency over the past twenty years, informal regional governance—in the form of voluntary cooperative arrangements between local governments, and in regional agenda setting efforts sponsored by civic organizations and non-profit planning organizations—has flourished.
>
> Informal governance often works where government fails because its structure is typically loose, its membership inclusive, and its strategies dependent on building cooperative coalitions. Whereas government is perceived as operating through a top-down approach to problems and imposing requirements on people, informal governance operates bottom-up by gathering authority from the people it can convince of its cause.

Box 3.10 Poor Children plus Middle-Class Schools
Equal Better Grades

"Integration works." That is the finding of a detailed study of the school performance of public housing children in Albuquerque. Conducted by the Urban Institute for the Carnegie Corporation of New York, the study examined test scores of 1,108 children from public housing households attending Albuquerque's elementary schools over a ten-year period.[1]

Albuquerque was chosen because it has an unusually high number of public housing children living in middle-class neighborhoods and attending middle-class neighborhood schools. Such social integration is the result of local government unity. With 80 percent of the metro area's population, Albuquerque is a near-metropolitan city. Its small, scattered-site public housing projects and rent subsidies cover almost all neighborhoods. And the Albuquerque public schools, the nation's twenty-fifth largest system, is one of only five metrowide school systems.

The results? Having controlled carefully for sex, race and ethnicity, and household characteristics, the study found that for every percentage point decrease in poverty among a public housing child's classmates, third grade test scores improved 0.22 percentile. In other words, attending a middle-class neighborhood school with 20 percent poor children rather than a poverty neighborhood school with 80 percent poor children meant a 13 percentile improvement in a public housing child's test scores!

1. David Rusk and Jeff Mosley, "The Academic Performance of Public Housing Children—Does Living in Middle Class Neighborhoods and Attending Middle Class Schools Make a Difference?" Urban Institute, Washington, D.C., May, 1994.

What is most impressive is that informal governance approaches to regionalism appear to be better able to address the difficult problems that elected officials either lack the courage or the will to address, for example, fair share housing, comprehensive regional land use and transportation planning, revenue base sharing, and tax increases."[4]

Since *Cities without Suburbs* was first published, I have worked with many such "regional civic organizations." Some have a "fair share" housing focus, such as the Connecticut Housing Coalition and Louisville's Metropolitan Housing Council. Others are concerned primarily with controlling urban sprawl, like New Jersey Future and 1,000 Friends of Oregon (though such groups quickly recognize that their communities are threatened by badly skewed human geography as well as environmental degradation). Good government groups may have deep historic roots (Chicago's Civic Federation) or be newly-organized (Rochester's Metropolitan Forum). Community leadership development programs are important forums for shaping tomorrow's leaders, like Leadership Metro Richmond, Leadership Greater Hartford, and Leadership Kentucky. Urban universities are intellectual goads for regional reform, such as Pace University, whose Law Institute is a prime mover for regional land use planning in New York; Virginia Commonwealth University, which provides strong support to Virginia's Urban Partnership; and Cleveland State University, which has spearheaded pathbreaking research on the adverse impact of federal capital gains taxation on many older urban communities. And local foundations, such as Baltimore's Abell Foundation, Pittsburgh's Heinz Endowments, the Saint Paul Foundation, and the Community Foundation of Greater New Haven, are constantly backing reform movements.

But by far the most consistent force for regional reform around the country is business organizations. Business is regionalism's natural constituency. With the globalization of manufacturing, the historic ties between many multinational industries and their home communities may have weakened, and one-third of retail businesses are now national chains and franchises with shallower local roots. Yet the very lifeblood of important business interests—banks, utilities, newspapers and broadcasters, contractors and developers, and hospitals among others—is dependent on their region's social and economic success. Business people view customers and employees without jurisdictional blinders and are more innoculated against excessive turf protection than local elected officials (and, indeed, than many local residents).

Chambers of commerce are almost invariably organized to serve entire metropolitan areas. Private economic development alliances such as the thirteen-county, bistate Carolinas Partnership, are increasingly common. After a half century, the granddaddy of regional business groups, the Pittsburgh area's Allegheny Conference on Community Development, remains one of the most dynamic and effective (see Box 3.11).

Box 3.11 Business Alliance Spearheads Pittsburgh's Regional Reforms

With 130 fiercely independent small suburban cities surrounding Pittsburgh, Allegheny County seems an unlikely place for regionalism. Yet the proposal for an Allegheny Regional Asset District was an instant winner with the Pennsylvania General Assembly.[1] The District was approved by the legislature in December 1993 and subsequently activated by vote of the Allegheny County Commissioners.

Administered by an independent, seven-member board, half of the revenues from the district's 1 percent, countywide sales tax will support regional parks, libraries, the Pittsburgh Zoo, Three Rivers Stadium, and other regional cultural facilities. The other half of the revenue will be divided between county and municipal governments—at least two-thirds, the legislature specified, to reduce other local taxes, such as property taxes.

The Regional Asset District was just the latest success of the Allegheny Conference on Community Development and its affiliated Pennsylvania Economy League. Founded in 1943, the Allegheny Conference has at its core a thirty-five-member executive committee that brings together most of the chief executives of the Pittsburgh area's largest corporations. The Allegheny Conference's first great achievement was cleaning up Pittsburgh's soot-shrouded skies in the decade after World War II. The conference also spearheaded Renaissance I, which created the Golden Triangle, Pittsburgh's downtown core, and Renaissance II, which spawned many cultural and sports facilities. The Allegheny Conference's greatest challenge was to help remake the Pittsburgh area's economy after 80,000 steel industry jobs were lost in the early 1980s. Now it has made reforming and improving public governance its top priority.

"The creation of the Allegheny Regional Asset District is a truly historic achievement for southwestern Pennsylvania," the conference has commented. "It represents the most significant improvement in the structure of our government in forty years."

1. Information from *Regional Directions* (Pittsburgh, Pa.: Allegheny Conference on Community Development, March 1994).

Some knowledgeable observers believe that regional *government* is impossible, but that regional *governance* is the wave of the future. "The past emphasis on structural regionalism, rendered infeasible by political considerations, has given way to a third wave, characterized by cross-sectoral alliances . . . [s]ustained by rich networks of affiliations among public, private, and nonprofit organizations."[5] In some respects, the difference may be largely semantic. Whether the goal is to create more unified formal governmental structures or get existing, fragmented structures to act more in unison, the focus is on changing public policy. However, formal structural change is more enduring. Voluntary citizen alliances do not have the multidecade staying power of formal structural reforms. Nevertheless, such extragovernmental reform movements are precisely what is needed to build political support for metro government.

Unprodded by citizen pressure, few state houses show any willingness to shoulder the tough political task of metropolitan reorganization. Mayors, city councillors, and county commissioners are too caught up in short-term pressures for survival and too politically comfortable with existing divisions. The National Civic League has correctly noted that most local governments "have assiduously avoided policies and arrangements which would result in sharing the social burdens of inner city populations or otherwise breaching the social insulation of the suburbs from their central city problems."[6]

The battleground is the state legislature. Such "regional civic organizations" must be the footsoldiers of regional reform.

Notes

1. A special definition must be created for the gigantic, multistate New York-northwestern New Jersey-Long Island CMSA. Within the New York portion, the New York PMSA, Nassau-Suffolk PMSA, and Orange County PMSA should be considered as one combined area. Within this area a Class III metropolitan government should serve 75 percent or more; and a Class II, 90 percent or more. The New Jersey and Connecticut components can be treated under the regular definitions.

2. The definitive study is *The IRS Homeseller Capital Gain Provision: Contributor to Urban Decline*, Ohio Housing Research Network, Ohio Urban University Program.

3. Neighborhood safety, schools, taxes and services, and other factors influence family decisions about where to live; no assessment has been made about the relative importance of capital gains tax concerns.

4. National Civic League, "Regional Civic Governance: Emerging Organizational Structure and Strategies: A Proposal by the National Civic League," *National Civic Review* (August 1991): 3.

5. Allan D. Walls, "The Third Wave: Current Trends in Regional Governance," *National Civic Review* (Summer/Fall 1994).

6. National Civic League, "Regional Civic Governance," 3.

Chapter IV

Conclusions and Recommendations

What is missing from current debate over urban policy is any willingness to attack the urban problem as a matter of racial and economic segregation. Liberals appeal for large-scale federal aid for social welfare and economic development programs in the inner cities. This is the Big Buck Strategy. Conservatives talk about inner city enterprise zones, public housing "perestroika," and "empowerment." This is the Big Bootstrap Strategy.

At heart, Big Buckers and Big Bootstrappers are selling the same idea: quarantine "them" in inner-city ghettos and barrios away from "us" and help "them" build from within—with money or moral incentives. Both ideological camps believe that separate can be made equal, or at least equal enough to be tolerable.

"Separate but equal" cannot work. It has never worked. Ghettos and barrios create and perpetuate an urban underclass. *Bad communities defeat good programs.* Successful clients of social programs typically move away. As a result, in inner cities, individual success does not translate into community success. Life in ghettos and barrios gets worse. Even with flourishing downtowns, inner cities decline. Inner-city neighborhoods deteriorate as places to raise families. With shrinking tax bases, city budgets are unable to meet rising social needs.

Enterprise zones, community development banks, nonprofit inner-city housing developments—all the tools of "empowerment"—are not futile efforts. They will produce some new businesses, some new jobs, some new homes, and some revitalized neighborhoods. They will be more effective, however, if carried out within a framework of actions to bring down the walls between city and suburb. Absent efforts at reunification, such programs will be unable to reverse the downward slide of the inner cities.

127

National urban policy, state-by-state urban policy, and area-by-area urban policy must focus on breaking up ghettos and barrios. Urban policy must systematically help ghetto and barrio residents become integrated into the entire metropolitan area. A revived middle class in the cities—not a "bucked-up" or "boot-strapped-up" urban poor—must be the leavening yeast of inner city revival.

Urban underclass behavior substantially dissolves with integration into the larger community. Individual poverty and dependency or individual acts of crime certainly do not disappear, but they lack critical mass to blight whole communities. Within all metro areas the proportion of poor minorities, if dispersed, is not so large as to overwhelm middle-class culture. It is the very isolation and hyperconcentration of poor minorities that overwhelms them individually. Neither poor people nor inner cities can succeed if they are cast into the sociological equivalents of giant public housing projects.

Throughout history cities have been the arena of opportunity and upward mobility. In America the "city" has been redefined since World War II. The real city is now the whole urban area—city and suburb—the metropolitan area. Redeeming inner cities and the urban underclass requires reintegration of city and suburb.

This is the toughest political issue in American society. It goes right to the heart of Americans' fears about race and class. There will be no short-term, politically comfortable solutions.

The organization of metro areas into local governments has greatly affected the degree of racial and economic segregation. Within their expanding municipal boundaries, elastic cities have captured much of the growth of the suburbs. Elastic cities minimize city-suburb disparities, thereby lessening the separations between racial and economic groups.

Inelastic cities, in the battle over middle-class America, have lost to their suburbs. Some never even fought the good fight. Whatever the success of their downtowns as regional employment centers, inelastic city neighborhoods have increasingly housed most of the metro area's poor Blacks and Hispanics.

How can responsibility for poor minorities be made a metropolitan-wide responsibility? How can all jurisdictions—city and suburb—assume a "fair share"?

Traditionally, the primary purpose of regional cooperation among local governments has been the delivery of public services. Regional arrangements usually avoid policies and programs that share the social burdens of inner-city residents. Yet this is the heart of the challenge. Areawide compacts on transportation planning, solid-waste management, sewage treatment, and air quality management may be "good government," but they address the urban problem only if they attack racial and economic segregation.

For many small and medium-sized metro areas, the surest way to avoid or reverse patterns of racial and economic segregation is to create metro governments. This can be achieved by expanding the central city through aggressive annexation policies, by consolidating the city and county, or by fully empowering county government and abolishing or reducing the role of municipalities.

For larger, more complex metro areas, metro government may be neither politically feasible nor administratively desirable. Larger government is not necessarily more efficient government. At any scale, efficiency is largely a function of good management. Given the bureaucratic impulse of many large systems, metro government may be less efficient and less responsive as a deliverer of services than smaller governments.

It is not important that local residents have their garbage picked up by a metrowide garbage service or their parks managed by a metrowide parks and recreation department. It is important that all local governments pursue common policies that will diminish racial and economic segregation. The following four policies are essential:

1. "fair share" housing policies (supported by planning and zoning policies) that will encourage low- and moderate-income housing in all jurisdictions;
2. fair employment and fair housing policies to ensure full access by minorities to the job and housing markets;
3. housing assistance policies to disperse low-income families to small-unit, scattered-site housing projects and to rent-subsidized private rental housing throughout a diversified metro housing market; and
4. tax-sharing arrangements that will offset tax-base disparities between the central city and its suburbs.

In baldest terms, sustained success requires moving poor people from bad city neighborhoods to good suburban neighborhoods and moving dollars from relatively wealthy suburban governments to poorer city governments. The long-term payoffs will be an overall reduction in poverty, dependency, and crime areawide, and "prosperous cities [which] are the key to vital regional economies and to safe and healthy suburbs."[1]

State government must play the leading role. Local government is the creature of state government, which sets the ground rules for local initiative and can create new local governments and merge old ones. Furthermore, governors and state legislators can and do act as metrowide policymakers. State government also plays an increasingly important role in revenue sharing for local government. With the purse comes additional power (and responsibility) to make the organization of metro areas more rational and equitable.

State government must act. It must

1. improve annexation laws to facilitate continuous central city expansion into urbanizing areas;
2. enact laws to encourage city-county consolidation or to reorganize local government by direct state statute;
3. in highly balkanized states, empower county governments so that they can act as de facto metro governments;
4. require all local governments in metro areas to have "fair share" affordable housing laws;
5. establish metrowide tax-sharing arrangements for local governments or utilize state aid as revenue equalizers; and
6. enact strong statewide growth management laws to curb urban sprawl.

As I stated earlier, reorganizing local government is primarily a task for initiative and hard work at the state and local levels. There are key roles, however, for the federal government. Since World War II the federal government's "urban policy" has been "suburban policy." It is past time for the federal government to deal with the consequences of its handiwork in terms of helping bridge the city-suburb gap.

First, the federal government should focus federal research and evaluation on integrating poor minorities into social mainstream communities. This is preferable to aiding them through social programs for socially isolated inner-city areas.

Second, the federal government should utilize the U.S. Advisory Commission on Intergovernmental Relations more actively. The commission could help the National Governors Association,

National Conference of State Legislators, National Association of Counties, National League of Cities, and other organizations promote metropolitan reorganization and develop model state laws.

Third, each federal program should be reviewed to see whether it increases or diminishes racial and economic segregation. This could be done by the Domestic Council or similar White House led body. Executive regulations or congressional amendments should then modify federal programs to diminish segregating effects and increase integrating effects.

Fourth, the federal government should initiate a major reform of the federal public housing program. Local public housing authorities should be made metrowide and should emphasize the use of rent-subsidy vouchers to provide access for the city poor to rental housing throughout metro areas. Housing the urban poor in high-density, inner-city public housing projects is patently destructive and should be ended as soon as possible.

Fifth, enforcement of federal laws on fair employment and fair housing should be made more vigorous.

Finally, the federal government should determine whether public and private policies that result in economic segregation, because of their high correlation with racial segregation, are *de facto* violations of federal civil rights laws.

On entering the White House, President Clinton set his priorities as revitalizing the economy, controlling health care costs, and reducing the federal budget deficit. Although these are daunting tasks, there are still a greater national consensus and more policy tools at hand to address these priorities than there is willingness to attack the schisms between city and suburb that lie at the core of America's urban problem.

Sustained change will require a grassroots movement like the civil rights movement or the environmental movement. This new movement will be tougher to begin. The civil rights movement in the 1960s mobilized moral outrage against Jim Crow laws. The environmental movement in the 1970s reflected compelling concern with human survival on a despoiled planet. But for the movement against urban segregation to get off the ground in the 1990s, a climate of perception, a climate of support, and a climate of change must all be created.

Over 80 percent of all minorities now live in America's metropolitan areas. A racially equitable society can be achieved only if urban America is changed. Conversely, solving the problems of cities requires addressing the city-suburb schisms that have intensified since World War II.

This is a journey on which few may initially choose to embark. But consider some of the alternative choices.

In an increasingly global economy would we choose to sacrifice the talent and productivity of inner-city residents and burden society with growing costs of dependency and social disruption?

In a capital-scarce society would we choose to discard the tremendous investment in the inner cities?

In a world of fragile interdependence would we choose to have many suburbs survive as independent and prosperous communities while the inner cities collapse at the metropolitan core?

In a world in which the technology of violence can touch anyone, would we choose to live in a garrison state where police power tries to seal off the have-nots from the haves?

These "choices" suggest where the racial and economic segregation of urban America is leading. The crisis requires not just urban aid or even a true "urban policy" but a commitment to a spirit of shared sacrifice and renewal. The crisis requires exchanging the old politics of exclusion for a new politics of inclusion. It will test whether or not the American people can develop a new spirit of community.

Afterword

"You may have shifted from a theme of cities without suburbs to suburbs with incidental cities," commented my colleague Hank Savitch after reviewing an early draft of this book.

> Your central argument is that cities 'succeed' only if they continue to absorb suburbs, which you see as America's preferred lifestyle. City survival ought not be so dependent upon imitating suburban patterns. How can cities become viable again within a metropolitan environment? Frankly, I believe that cities do have different roles to play.

His comments brought me up short. I love old-fashioned, bustling downtowns, and I love the old apartment buildings and town houses, nearby shops, tree-lined streets, mini-parks, buses, and subways of good urban neighborhoods. There is nothing sadder than a city that undertakes a redevelopment project that looks and functions like a suburban office park and shopping mall.

As mayor I often spoke of Albuquerque as "a giant suburb in search of a city." Albuquerque had all the suburban lifestyle its advocates could possibly want, I suggested. Albuquerque needed to strengthen its urban character. With modest success and much controversy, I promoted downtown Albuquerque as a center of business, government, entertainment, and the arts.

Having returned to Washington, D.C., we live again in the District of Columbia in a condominium twelve minutes from the White House. A Metro bus stop is at the front door and a city park at the back door. Yet the District of Columbia is today only 15 percent of the population of the 4-million-person Washington Metropolitan Area, even before the census experts merged it with the 2.5-million-person Baltimore Metropolitan Area in 1992 to create the nation's fourth largest urban region.

133

Twenty years ago Washingtonians never went to Baltimore. There was nothing there. Today, Baltimore's spectacular Inner Harbor is a standard weekend attraction. At wonderful Camden Yards baseball park, one-third of the Orioles' 3.5 million fans come from the Washington area.

Both Washington, D.C., and Baltimore play their roles as regional centers very well as do, for example, Atlanta, Boston, Minneapolis, San Francisco, and much-maligned New York City. There is one regional role, however, in which these cities cannot succeed—and that may ultimately crush them. They cannot continue as human warehouses for most of their metro areas' poor minorities. However glittering their downtowns, many of their neighborhoods are slowly dying.

The erosion is not so much physical. Many older neighborhoods in Washington, D.C., are physically very attractive—an urban regentrifier's paradise. It is the social chemistry that has gone awry.

I hope that no one who has read to this point still interprets my arguments as being primarily a plea for fiscal equity—that suburbs should pay the bill for cities to take care of the problems of the metro area's poor. There is no amount of money that can feasibly be spent to accomplish that. "Bad neighborhoods defeat good programs," I have stated. "Ghettos can only become bigger ghettos."

The severity of the social chaos in many inner-city neighborhoods—unemployment, poverty, dependency, illegitimacy, drugs, crime—is a function of the intense concentration and isolation of the minority poor. The misery of the whole is much greater than the sum of individual hardships. Inner cities should not have to assume the role of sole providers for the minority poor. That must become the responsibility of the whole metro area—city and suburbs, cities without suburbs.

Fifteen years ago I argued these themes at the U.S. Conference of Mayors. I got virtually no support. Suburban mayors did not want to think about central cities. They believed their constituents had said goodbye and good riddance to the city. Central city mayors—more and more, Black or Hispanic—did not want to hear any proposals that might threaten their political comfort levels. After all, Black and Hispanic communities had waited a long time to achieve real power at city hall.

Today the need for radical action is much more acute, yet the choruses of "empowerment" continue to swell. I am not unsympathetic. But a vision rises before my eyes. The *Titanic* has just hit the iceberg. The captain turns to his long-time first mate and says, "Here. You take charge. I'm outta here." It is a pretty empty promotion for the first mate. It is also no consolation to the poor people stowed away in steerage who cannot get off the sinking ship.

My metaphor is exaggerated. Being mayor of a major city is no empty honor or responsibility. Cities are still important, and having Black and Hispanic mayors is important for the entire society.

The solution, however, is not to watch from the safety of the *Carpathia* as the great ship goes down. Help get many of the people in steerage into the lifeboats. Keep a top-flight crew on board to repair the tears in the ship's fabric and recruit more adventuresome, well-heeled passengers to come back on board again. Promote the former first mate to admiral of the fleet.

Throughout this book I have not focused enough on one key element of solving the urban problem: what to do about inner-city public schools. Many middle-class families make decisions about where to live largely based on the quality of local schools. Inner-city neighborhoods can be repeopled with childless middle-class households if neighborhoods are made safer. Re-attracting middle-class households with children to raise into many city neighborhoods requires dramatic improvements in schools. And, of course, the children who are already in inner-city schools most need and deserve better schools.

In no way have I meant to ignore the challenge nor to downgrade the central importance of the quality of local schools in city revival. But the mix of children in the classroom is another of the issues that is no longer discussed in Washington. Most proposals to reform urban education strike me as another version of the nonargument between Big Buckers and Big Bootstrappers over urban policy. By contrast, I believe that the major path to school reform lies in integration—racial and economic— of metropolitan housing markets.

One final observation. Metro government will strike many people as smacking of Big Brother. In many ways the belief that "smaller government is better government" resonates emotionally within me as well.

As Albuquerque grew, more and more residents felt the loss of the small-town atmosphere they had treasured. One of my antidotes to "bigness" was to encourage "smallness." City hall actively promoted the growth of neighborhood associations. From nineteen neighborhood associations when I took office, the neighborhood movement grew to over ninety associations four years later.

Most neighborhood associations are like army reserve units. They have their community picnics in local parks once or twice a year (like two weeks of summer encampment), but they are not mass movements year-round. They are kept alive by a small cadre of dedicated activists, but they are there to provide a framework for mass mobilization when a crisis occurs.

In city life a neighborhood crisis most often happens when neighbors believe that someone is going to do something to the neighborhood: a developer proposes an apartment building on the edges of a single-family home neighborhood, or the city government plans to put a drug-treatment center in an old mansion, or—the nuclear war of city planning—the state highway department revives old plans for a freeway right through the area.

Faced with almost any proposed change in the area, neighborhood associations are profoundly conservative. They are typically against any proposal for well-enumerated reasons. Months of meetings and public hearings usually follow. Ultimately, if the proposal is not killed by neighborhood opposition, the final result is a modified plan that is generally better, on balance, than the original project.

Any forward progress, however, requires a willingness by the planning commission, the city council, and the mayor to push forward for what is in the interests of the larger community. If left strictly to the preferences of the neighborhood association (and the city councillor from that area), *nothing* would ever happen.

What has happened in much of urban America is analogous. In many areas public responsibility and public accountability have become so fragmented that nobody can act for the good of the larger community. In so many metro areas, local government has become little but an agglomeration of large-scale neighborhood associations. No overall planning commission or city council or mayor has a comprehensive vision and the courage to act for all. It is time for governors and state legislators to step into that void.

Note

1. Bill Clinton and Al Gore, *Putting People First: How We Can All Change America* (New York: Times Books, 1992), p. 52.

Appendix

Central Cities and Metro Areas by Elasticity Category

This appendix ranks central cities by their relative elasticity within the different categories outlined in Chapter II for metropolitan areas. Both central cities and metropolitan areas are listed as defined for the 1990 census. The cities are ranked in ascending order of elasticity. The most inelastic city is ranked first in the "zero elasticity" column. The most elastic city will be listed last in the "hyper elasticity" column.

These rankings are often more art than exact science. Cities with sharply different circumstances can sometimes have the same elasticity score. I have generally given the edge to rate of expansion in municipal area rather than initial residential density. Readers should not get caught up in slight differences in elasticity rankings among cities, but focus on where each city falls among the broad categories.

In each table a city that is in uppercase letters (for example, OAKLAND, Calif.) is considered to be the primary or historic central city for that metro area. A city in lowercase (for example, Berkeley, Calif.) is considered to be a secondary central city. In all instances where two or more central cities are designated in a metro area's title, I have chosen the first named. Thus, MINNEAPOLIS, Minnesota, is the primary central city and St. Paul, Minnesota, is the secondary central city.

An asterisk (*) following a city's name indicates that the city was already considered a central city in the 1950 census.

TABLE A-1

145 CENTRAL CITIES OVER 100,000 POPULATION IN 117 LARGE METRO AREAS[a]

Zero Elasticity	Low Elasticity	Medium Elasticity	High Elasticity	Hyper Elasticity
NEW YORK, N.Y.*	WORCESTER, Mass.*	GARY, Ind.	ALBUQUERQUE, N.M.*	Arlington, Tex.
NEWARK, N.J.*	SPRINGFIELD, Mass.*	DES MOINES, Iowa*	DALLAS, Tex.*	LITTLE ROCK, Ark.*
PATERSON, N.J.	MIAMI, Fla.*	Hialeah, Fla.	MODESTO, Calif.	VALLEJO, Calif.
BOSTON, Mass.*	OAKLAND, Calif.*	TOLEDO, Ohio*	MADISON, Wisc.*	Kansas City, Kans.
ST. LOUIS, Mo.*	ALBANY, N.Y.*	EVANSVILLE, Ind.*	KANSAS CITY, Mo.*	TAMPA, Fla.*
PROVIDENCE, R.I.*	ALLENTOWN, Pa.*	St. Petersburg, Fla.*	MACON, Ga.*	TULSA, Okla.*
DETROIT, Mich.*	Arlington, Va.	ANAHEIM, Calif.	COLUMBUS, Ohio*	GREENSBORO, N.C.*
WASHINGTON, D.C.*	Portsmouth, Va.*	LANSING, Mich.*	SACRAMENTO, Calif.*	ORLANDO, Fla.*
PITTSBURGH, Pa.*	Waterbury, Conn.*	DENVER, Colo.*	SANTA ROSA, Calif.	MONTGOMERY, Ala.*
CLEVELAND, Ohio*	NEW ORLEANS, La.*	OMAHA, Nebr.*	San Bernardino, Calif.*	FRESNO, Calif.*
BALTIMORE, Md.*	TACOMA, Wash.*	PEORIA, Ill.*	FORT WORTH, Tex.*	RALEIGH, N.C.*
HARTFORD, Conn.*	HONOLULU, Hawaii	BIRMINGHAM, Ala.*	SAN DIEGO, Calif.*	TALLAHASSEE, Fla.
Elizabeth, N.J.	Pasadena, Calif.	SALINAS, Calif.	SHREVEPORT, La.*	Newport News, Va.
MINNEAPOLIS, Minn.*	Hampton, Va.	FORT WAYNE, Ind.*	Irving, Tex.	LEXINGTON, Ky.*
ROCHESTER, N.Y.*	Stamford, Conn.*	ANN ARBOR, Mich.	LAS VEGAS, Nev.	CORPUS CHRISTI, Tex.*
NEW HAVEN, Conn.*	LOS ANGELES, Calif.*	Hollywood, Fla.	HUNTSVILLE, Ala.	NASHVILLE, Tenn.*
SYRACUSE, N.Y.*	ERIE, Pa.*	Pomona, Calif.	Winston Salem, N.C.*	LUBBOCK, Tex.*
Lowell, Mass.*	SEATTLE, Wash.*	FORT LAUDERDALE, Fla.	CHATTANOOGA, Tenn.*	RENO, Nev.
JERSEY CITY, N.Y.*	MILWAUKEE, Wis.*	Tempe, Ariz.		COLUMBUS, Ga.*
	FLINT, Mich.*	RIVERSIDE, Calif.		

CHICAGO, Ill.*	LOUISVILLE, Ky.*	Santa Ana, Calif.	WICHITA, Kans.*	PHOENIX, Ariz.*
SAN FRANCISCO, Calif.*	AKRON, Ohio*	ROCKFORD, Ill.*	HOUSTON, Tex.*	JACKSONVILLE, Fla.*
PHILADELPHIA, Pa.*	Long Beach, Calif.	OXNARD, Calif.	STOCKTON, Calif.*	AUSTIN, Tex.*
BUFFALO, N.Y.*	GRAND RAPIDS, Mich.*	MEMPHIS, Tenn.*	SAN ANTONIO, Tex.*	SAN JOSE, Calif.*
Berkeley, Calif.	NORFOLK, Va.*	BATON ROUGE, La.*	JACKSON, Miss.*	Escondido, Calif.
BRIDGEPORT, Conn.*	RICHMOND, Va.*	LINCOLN, Nebr.*	MOBILE, Ala.*	Mesa, Ariz.
CINCINNATI, Ohio*	SOUTH BEND, Ind.*	ATLANTA, Ga.*	Durham, N.C.*	OKLAHOMA CITY, Okla.*
St. Paul, Minn.*	PORTLAND, Oreg.*	SAVANNAH, Ga.*	CHARLOTTE, N.C.*	BAKERSFIELD, Calif.
	DAYTON, Ohio*	BEAUMONT, Tex.*	INDIANAPOLIS, Ind.*	TUCSON, Ariz.
		Knoxville, Tenn.*		COLORADO SPRINGS, Colo.
				Virginia Beach, Va.
				ANCHORAGE, Alaska
				Scottsdale, Ariz.

Note: Cities in uppercase letters are considered to be the primary or historic central city for that metro area; cities in lowercase are considered to be secondary central cities.

[a]Metro areas with 200,000 or more residents in 1990.

*Cities already considered to be a central city in the 1950 census.

TABLE A-2
185 Central Cities under 100,000 Population in 48 Large Metro Areas[a]

Zero Elasticity	Low Elasticity	Medium Elasticity	High Elasticity	Hyper Elasticity
Hoboken, N.J.	Alliance, Ohio	Gloucester, Mass.	Baytown, Tex.	DAVENPORT, Iowa*
Cambridge, Mass.	Carlisle Brgh, Pa.	Bowling Green, Ohio	Delray Beach, Fla.	Gastonia, N.C.
TRENTON, N.J.*	East Chicago, Ind.	Mishawaka, Ind.	Slidell, La.	Bossier City, La.
Camden, N.J.	Waltham, Mass.	Moline, Ill.*	Elkhart, Ind.	DAYTONA BEACH, Fla.
Lawrence, Mass.*	Dearborn, Mich.	Belleville, Ill.	PENSACOLA, Fla.	Murfreesboro, Tenn.
WILMINGTON, Del.*	Hammond, Ind.	LORAIN, Ohio*	Chapel Hill, N.C.	Titusville, Fla.
Easton, Pa.*	Pontiac, Mich.	Lodi, Calif.	BOULDER, Colo.	GALVESTON, Tex.*
Lynn, Mass.	Bethlehem, Pa.*	Alton, Ill.	Texas City Tex.	CHARLESTON, S.C.*
Pawtucket, R.I.	East Lansing, Mich.	Woodland, Calif.	Jacksonville, Ark.	LAKELAND, Fla.
Perth Amboy, N.J.	Fall River, Mass.*	Davis, Calif.	Auburn, Wash.	Everett, Wash.
Schenectady, N.Y.	Norwalk, Conn.*	SANTA CRUZ, Calif.	ROANOKE, Va.*	High Point, N.C.*
Evanston, Ill.	Barberton, Ohio	Granite City, Ill.	Clearwater, Fla.	JOHNSON CITY, Tenn.
POUGHKEEPSIE, N.Y.	LANCASTER, Pa.*	Massillon, Ohio	Rock Hill, S.C.	Kingsport, Tenn.
Norristown Brgh, Pa.	Brockton, Mass.*	HAMILTON, Ohio*	Marietta, Ga.	COLUMBIA, S.C.*
NEW BRUNSWICK, N.J.	Holyoke, Mass.*	Bristol, Va.	Livermore, Calif.	Norman, Okla.
Miami Beach, Fla.	SARASOTA, Fla.	BLOOMINGTON, Ill.	Tulare, Calif.	Suffolk, Va.
Lebanon, Pa.	North Chicago, Ill.	Porterville, Calif.	Petersburg, Va.	FAYETTEVILLE, N.C.
UTICA, N.Y.*	Kannapolis, N.C.	GREENVILLE, S.C.*	HICKORY, N.C.	WEST PALM BEACH, Fla.
East St. Louis, Ill.	Milford, Conn.	Elgin, Ill.	Warner Robins, Ga.	Bessemer, Ala.
Woonsocket, R.I.	Meriden, Conn.	Lompoc, Calif.	FORT MYERS, Fla.	
	Fitchburg, Mass.	Turlock, Calif.	Leavenworth, Kans.	
	Bristol, Conn.*	West Memphis, Ark.	Bristol, Tenn.	

NEW BEDFORD, Mass.*
SAGINAW, Mich.*
Bay City, Mich.*
New Britain, Conn.*
ATLANTIC CITY, N.J.*
Salem, Mass.
McKeesport, Pa.
YORK, Pa.*
HARRISBURG, Pa.*
READING, Pa.*
YOUNGSTOWN, Ohio*
NEW LONDON, Conn.
Port Huron, Mich.
Burbank, Calif.
White Plains, N.Y.
Monterey, Calif.
Troy, N.Y.*
NIAGARA FALLS, N.Y.
Annapolis, Md.

Norwich, Conn.
Framingham, Mass.
Rock Island, Ill.*
Bloomington, Minn.
CANTON, Ohio*
Chicago Heights, Ill.
Oak Ridge, Tenn.
Leominster, Mass.
Northampton, Mass.
Attleboro, Mass.
Rome, N.Y.*
Middleton, Conn.
Westfield, Mass.
SANTA BARBARA, Calif.
FORT PIERCE, Fla.
Kent, Ohio
Pekin, Ill.
Springfield, Ohio*
AUGUSTA, Ga.*
Haverhill, Mass.
Warren, Ohio
New Albany, Ind.
Petaluma, Calif.

Lancaster, Ohio
Spartanburg, S.C.
Newark, Ohio
KALAMAZOO, Mich.*
Seaside, Calif.
Longmont, Colo.
Winter Haven, Fla.
WAUKEGAN, Ill.
Elyria, Ohio*
BRADENTON, Fla.
Ventura, Calif.
Santa Maria, Calif.
Napa, Calif.
St. Charles, Mo.
JOLIET, Ill.
Frederick, Md.

Palo Alto, Calif.
VISALIA, Calif.
Pompano Beach, Fla.
Council Bluffs, Iowa
Boca Raton, Fla.
Palm Springs, Calif.
MELBOURNE, Fla.
AURORA, Ill.
North Little Rock, Ark.*
Midland, Mich.

Danbury, Conn.
Fairfield, Calif.
KILEEN, Tex.
LAFAYETTE, La.*
Port Arthur, Tex.*
GAINESVILLE, Fla.
Shawnee, Okla.
Roseville, Calif.
Denton, Tex.
Temple, Tex.
Olathe, Kans.
Palm Bay, Fla.

Note: Cities in uppercase letters are considered to be the primary or historic central city for that metro area; cities in lowercase are considered to be secondary central cities.

aMetro areas with 200,000 or more residents in 1990.

*Cities already considered to be a central city in the 1950 census.

TABLE A-3

144 CENTRAL CITIES UNDER 100,000 POPULATION IN 122 SMALL METRO AREAS[a]

Zero Elasticity	Low Elasticity	Medium Elasticity	High Elasticity	Hyper Elasticity
ELMIRA, N.Y.	RACINE, Wis.*	FLORENCE, S.C.	PUEBLO, Colo.*	LONGVIEW, Tex.
SHARON, Pa.	SHEBOYGAN, Wis.	CASPER, Wyo.	Pasco, Wash.	RICHLAND, Wash.
STATE COLLEGE, Pa.	KOKOMO, Ind.	Hopkinsville, Ky.	ST. JOSEPH, Mo.*	GREEN BAY, Wis.*
GLEN FALLS, N.Y.	LAFAYETTE, Ind.	NAPLES, Fla.	SPRINGFIELD, Ill.*	RAPID CITY, S. Dak.
JAMESTOWN, N.Y.	HOUMA, La.	ST. CLOUD, Minn.	Kennewick, Wash.	ROCHESTER, Minn.
JACKSON, Mich.*	PANAMA CITY, Fla.	DOTHAN, Ala.	DECATUR, Ala.	Lynchburg, Va.
BENTON HARBOR, Mich.	GADSDEN, Ala.*	SANTA FE, N.M.	ASHEVILLE, N.C.*	BILLINGS, Mont.
Dunkirk, N.Y.	FORT WALTON BEACH, Fla.	TERRE HAUTE, Ind.	Bismarck, N. Dak.	PINE BLUFF, Ark.
Bridgeton, N.J.	Moorhead, Minn.	DUBUQUE, Iowa	DECATUR, Ill.*	GREELEY, Colo.
Rantoul Village, Ill.	KANKAKEE, Ill.	PASCAGOULA, Miss.	VICTORIA, Tex.	BATTLE CREEK, Mich.
Thibodaux, La.	YUBA CITY, Calif.	Normal Town, Ill.	MIDLAND, Tex.	TUSCALOOSA, Ala.
HAGERSTOWN, Md.	YAKIMA, Wash.	BURLINGTON, N.C.	WILMINGTON, N.C.	FARGO, N. Dak.
West Lafayette, Ind.	CHARLOTTES-VILLE, Va.	ATHENS, Ga.	BRYAN, Tex.	JACKSON, Tenn.
BURLINGTON, Vt.	SIOUX CITY, Iowa*	MEDFORD, Oreg.	Waco, Tex.*	DANVILLE, Va.
Lima, Ohio*	BANGOR, Maine	FLORENCE, Ala.	CHICO, Calif.	ABILENE, Tex.
Urbana, Ill.	KENOSHA, Wisc.*	BREMERTON, Wash.	SIOUX FALLS, S. Dak.*	JACKSONVILLE, N.C.
MUSKEGON, Mich.	OWENSBORO, Ky.	TEXARKANA, Tex.	Springdale, Ark.	LAS CRUCES, N.M.
ANDERSON, S.C.	BLOOMINGTON, Ind.	Gulfport, Miss.	TYLER, Tex.	Cedar Falls, Iowa
Millville, N.J.	MONROE, La.	LAKE CHARLES, La.	Wichita Falls, Tex.*	ODESSA, Tex.
BELLINGHAM, Wash.	GREAT FALLS, Mont.	JOPLIN, Mo.	ANDERSON, Ind.	SHERMAN, Tex.
		ELKHART, Ind.	AMARILLO, Tex.*	FAYETTEVILLE, Ark.
		FORT SMITH, Ark.	MANSFIELD, Ohio	

Pittsfield, Mass.*	LAWRENCE, Kans.	CHEYENNE, Wyo.	TOPEKA, Kans.*	Columbia, Mo.
LEWISTON, Maine*	BLOOMINGTON, Ill.	ALEXANDRIA, La.		FORT COLLINS, Colo.
VINELAND, N.J.	Goshen, Ind.	SAN ANGELO, Tex.*		Loveland, Colo.
Auburn, Maine	Beloit, Wis.	JANESVILLE, Wis.		ENID, Okla.
CHAMPAIGN, Ill.	BILOXI, Miss.	ANNISTON, Ala.		LAWTON, Okla.
	GRAND FORKS, N. Dak.	Texarkana, Ark.		REDDING, Calif.
	EAU CLAIRE, Wis.	YUMA, Ariz.		ALBANY, Ga.
	LA CROSSE, Wis.	MERCED, Calif.		College Station, Tex.
	WAUSAU, Wis.	WATERLOO, Iowa*		OCALA, Fla.
	MUNCIE, Ind.*	MARSHALL, Tex.		CLARKSVILLE, Tenn.
		CEDAR RAPIDS, Iowa*		
		Denison, Tex.		
		OLYMPIA, Wash.		
		IOWA CITY, Iowa		

Note: Cities in uppercase letters are considered to be a primary or historic central city for that metro area; cities in lowercase are considered to be secondary central cities.

a Metro areas with fewer than 200,000 residents.

*Cities already considered to be a central city in the 1950 census.

TABLE A-4
FOUR SPECIAL CATEGORIES

Zero Elasticity	Low Elasticity	Medium Elasticity	High Elasticity	Hyper Elasticity
		Mexican Border Towns in 4 Metro Areas		
Pharr, Tex.	Harlingen, Tex.	Mission, Tex.		McALLEN, Tex.
	Edinburg, Tex.	LAREDO, Tex.*		EL PASO, Tex.*
		BROWNSVILLE, Tex.		
		Declining Mining Regions		
JOHNSTOWN, Pa.*	Weirton, W. Va.	DULUTH, Minn.*		
Wilkes-Barre, Pa.*	WHEELING, W. Va.*	CHARLESTON, W. Va.*		
ALTOONA, Pa.*	Ashland, Ky.*			
HUNTINGTON, W. Va.*	Superior, Wis.*			
Hazleton, Pa.*	Marietta, Ohio			
SCRANTON, Pa.*	PARKERSBURG, W. Va.			
WILLIAMSPORT, Pa.				
CUMBERLAND, Md.				
STEUBENVILLE, Ohio*				

White-America Cities in 13 Metro Areas

BINGHAMPTON, N.Y.*

PORTLAND, Maine*
PORTSMOUTH, N.H.
Neenah, Wis.
Nashua, N.H.
Dover, N.H.
Rochester, N.H.
MANCHESTER, N.H.*
Orem, Utah
VANCOUVER, Wash.
SPOKANE, Wash.*
Springfield, Oreg.

APPLETON, Wis.
Ogden, Utah
Oshkosh, Wis.
SALT LAKE CITY, Utah*

PROVO, Utah
SPRINGFIELD, Mo.*
SALEM, Oreg.

EUGENE, Oreg.
BOISE, Idaho

City-Less Metro Areas

NASSAU-SUFFOLK, N.Y.
MONMOUTH-OCEAN, N.J.
ORANGE COUNTY, N.Y.
BRAZORIA, Tex.
BEAVER VALLEY, Pa.

Note: Cities in uppercase letters are considered to be the primary or historic central city for that metro area; cities in lowercase are considered to be secondary central cities.

*Cities already considered to be a central city in the 1950 census.

Note from the Author

The research summarized in *Cities without Suburbs* is built upon a self-compiled database that, as hard copy, would equal the length of the book itself. To economize in length and cost, the publisher and I decided not to include the database as an appendix to this book.

However, I am eager to assist public officials, citizens, planning professionals, academic researchers, and students grappling with the complex problems of metropolitan areas.

Therefore, I have published separately the data by which I calculated the elasticity scores for all central cities as the *Cities without Suburbs Data Supplement*. For all 522 central cities the supplement will provide population density (1950 and 1990), percentage relative to national density average (1950), population density ranking by decile (1950), city area (1950 and 1990), city area expansion ranking by decile (1950–1990), elasticity score, and capture/contribute ratio.

The data supplement may be purchased for $20.00 per copy from David Rusk, 4100 Cathedral Avenue, NW, #610, Washington, D.C. 20016; phone (202) 364-2455; fax (202) 364-6936. I will also include a 3.5-inch diskette in either MacIntosh/Wingz or MS-DOS/Lotus 1-2-3 as requested.

Sources

All data not otherwise indicated are taken from publications of the Bureau of the Census of the U.S. Department of Commerce. These publications cover the decennial censuses from 1950 to 1990.

The sources for municipal bond ratings are *Moody's State and Local Government Data Book* (1991) and direct inquiries to city finance departments.

The calculations of residential segregation rates are drawn from Roderick J. Harrison and Daniel H. Weinberg, "Racial and Ethnic Segregation in 1990," U.S. Bureau of the Census, Washington, D.C., April 1992.

Similar calculations on school segregation have been made by Maris Mikelsons and Jeff Mosley of the Urban Institute and me. Our data come from tapes prepared by the National Center for Education Statistics of the U.S. Department of Education.

Per capita income data are drawn from the 1990 census, the Census Bureau's *State and Metropolitan Area Data Book 1991* and earlier editions (including the *City and County Data Book*). Based on census data, I have calculated suburban per capita incomes in 1989 myself.

All information on metro area employment trends, including manufacturing employment, comes from *Regional Projections to 2040: Volume 2 Metropolitan Statistical Areas*, published by the U.S. Commerce Department's Bureau of Economic Analysis (October 1990).

The analysis of state laws regarding city-county consolidation, municipal formation, and annexation powers is adapted from *State Laws Governing Local Government and Administration*, U.S. Advisory Commission on Intergovernmental Relations (March 1993). Table 1.8 is adapted from an earlier study of the same title by Melvin B. Hill, Jr., et al., published by the Institute of Government, University of Georgia (1971).

Information on changes in city minority population from 1980 to 1990 has been helpfully provided by Professor William H. Frey of the University of Michigan's Population Studies Center.

Information on regional civic organizations has been drawn from recent copies of the *National Civic Review,* published six times a year by the National Civic League. I have also quoted or paraphrased extensively from the NCL's proposal, "Regional Civic Governance: Emerging Organizational Structures and Strategies" (August 1991).

Finally, I am indebted to the inspiration provided by Professor Hank V. Savitch (University of Louisville), in particular "Ties That Bind: Central Cities, Suburbs, and the New Metropolitan Region" (unpublished paper). I also have referred to Hank V. Savitch, "The Regional City and Public Partnerships," in *In the National Interest: The 1990 Urban Summit,* The Twentieth Century Fund Press, New York, 1992. The material quoted in the Afterword is taken from personal correspondence from Dr. Savitch commenting on my manuscript.

Index

The Woodrow Wilson International Center for Scholars

The Center is the living memorial of the United States of America to the nation's twenty-eighth president, Woodrow Wilson. The U.S. Congress established the Woodrow Wilson Center in 1968 as an international institute for advanced study, "symbolizing and strengthening the fruitful relationship between the world of learning and the world of public affairs." The Center opened in 1970 under its own board of trustees.

Woodrow Wilson Center Special Studies

The work of the Center's Fellows, Guest Scholars, and staff—and presentations and discussions at the Center's conferences, seminars, and colloquia—often deserve timely circulation as contributions to public understanding of issues of national and international importance. The Woodrow Wilson Center Special Studies series makes such materials available to interested scholars, practitioners, and other readers. In all its activities, the Woodrow Wilson Center is a nonprofit, nonpartisan organization, supported financially by annual appropriations from the Congress, and by the contributions of foundations, corporations, and individuals. Conclusions or opinions expressed in Center publications and programs are those of the authors and speakers and do not necessarily reflect the views of the Center's staff, Fellows, trustees, advisory groups, or any individuals or organizations that provide financial support to the Center.